Romancing the Soul Along with the Heart: ®
The Secret of Lifelong Love

Written by:

FRANK HAJCAK, Ph.D.
&
TRICIA GARWOOD, MS

With:
JOY SHELTON

Cover Photo by:
Frank Hajcak

Illustrations by:
Frank Hajcak
Julie Vollmer

Human Potential Press
2011

Organizations and institutions that provide relationship enrichment services receive special generous discounted prices on bulk orders.
Contact:
 HumanPotentialPress@yahoo.com

Table of Contents

List of Poems

Illustrations

All photos © Frank Hajcak

All watercolors © JulieVollmer

Romancing the Soul along with the Heart,® is compatible with all faiths. Self directed individual couples craft the spiritual framework for courting their heart and soul together from their own religious, spiritual or meta-physical beliefs or affiliations. The activity, *Spiritual Seeds of Love,*® in session 18 on page 82 is an example of how spiritual beliefs add enjoyment, depth, intensity and longevity to romantic experiences.

In church sponsored group programs you can discuss any concerns you may have with the spiritual advisor.

Romancing the Soul along with the Heart®
Your Guide to Life Long Love

Overview

Romancing the Soul along with the Heart® systematically integrates your romantic thoughts, feelings and experiences into your spiritual framework to form a lifelong soul mate bond. Complete the 24 easy to follow sessions of the program and you will gain the power to shape and control your relationship, the power to create all the love you want and experience the **love centered life** described in detail on page 104. Follow the convenient **maintenance schedule** on page xiii and you will spend the rest of your life living in the moment of love that remains untarnished by events and undiminished by time. **This is not an empty promise.**

The **Warranty** on page xii certifies that all of the reflections and activities are based on the principles of cognitive-behavioral psychology which have a clinically proven success rate of 80-95%. They are effective and they will remain the cornerstone of psychology in the 21st century.

How It Works

When you romance the soul and the heart together you experience the personal intensity of your romantic feelings simultaneously with the depth, stability and sense of permanence of your spiritual beliefs. Thus, the two become integrated and influence one another. How**?**

Romantic, emotional experiences are anchored in the present and therefore have a very strong sense of immediacy and personal meaning. However, they are volatile, short lived and subject to the stress of daily living. Thus, they lack a long range perspective and a sense of permanence. If we lived by emotion alone life would be a roller coaster of fleeting, unstable relationships.

On the other hand, spiritual beliefs are abstract concepts anchored in the distant future (the afterlife) and therefore have a long term perspective. They are not subject to daily fluctuations and are relatively consistent throughout life. Therefore they have greater depth, stability and a sense of permanence. However, they lack the raw immediacy and the highly personalized meaning of emotional experiences.

Thus romantic experiences and spiritual beliefs must be combined and integrated in order to achieve a lifelong passionate relationship. Once they are integrated, emotional experiences acquire a stronger sense of stability and longevity. Conjointly, spiritual beliefs acquire a more intense sense of immediacy and personal meaning. Functioning as an integrated unit, emotional experiences and spiritual beliefs, transform a simple emotional bond into a profound lifelong soul mate bond. The enrichment activities of our program are designed to complete the integration process to form this bond.

HOW THIS MANUAL IS ORGANIZED

The Manual has 24 sessions. Each session begins with a brief excerpt adapted from ***Midnight Harvest: Living in the Moment of Love.*** Each introductory verse captures an experience couples will encounter on their journey to the lifelong soul mate bond. This is followed by a reflection on love and an activity which reconstructs the experience for you and your spouse to share.

- Session 1 focuses on taking ownership and responsibility for your relationship and gaining the power to change and control it.
- Sessions 2-8 focus on how to create an abundance of loving thoughts, feelings and experiences for courting the heart.
- Sessions 9-14 are devoted to removing the blocks which hinder the natural flow of the **Love Cycle**.
- Sessions 15-24 focus on courting the soul along with the heart to complete the soul mate bond.

Why poetry? Romantic poetic imagery with a spiritual framework is an ideal catalyst for bonding the heart with the soul. The spiritual aspect of the image courts the soul and lets you experience the depth, richness and sense of permanence of the spiritual realm. The romantic aspect of the image courts the heart and lets you experience the personal intensity of the emotional realm. In a few words, the image captures your heart and catapults you into the core of the soul mate bond with an intensity that would take pages and possibly even books of prose to accomplish.

USING THIS MANUAL

This manual can be used by individual couples or in group programs.

For individual couples:

- Find a private place where you won't be interrupted for approximately 30 minutes.
- One spouse reads the titled portion of the poem and the other reads the reply. Read as if you are gifting your spouse with words and feelings you have discovered in your own heart. The other spouse listens with an open heart to receive the gift.
- Next, share your thoughts, feelings and favorite lines or images with one another.
- Then, read aloud the **Reflection** on Love and complete the enrichment activity. Each activity is a tool designed to keep you moving on the path to lifelong love. Taking turns reading will build a spirit of cooperation and mutual commitment.
- After each activity, sign the pledge to follow the convenient maintenance schedule.
- Close each session after reading the **Afterthought** and discussing any questions, comments or ideas you may wish to share.
- **Remember**, doing an activity once produces a temporary positive effect. Expecting a single experience to transform your relationship into a lifelong soul mate bond is like buying a new car, filling the tank and expecting the gas to last the life of the car. **Please** read the section regarding maintenance schedules on the next page.
- **Keep in mind** that accepting and exercising responsibility for your relationship gives you the power to change and control it. Therefore, the more effort you put into each session and the follow up maintenance schedule, the more enrichment you will experience **and** the sooner you will achieve the love centered life described on page 104.

For groups:

- Before beginning each session have a volunteer give two 3x5 cards to each couple to use, if they so desire. Ask if there are any questions or comments on anything previously covered.
- Each session is preceded by guidelines for group leaders. In addition to these guidelines the group leader should read through the entire session prior to starting it. The instructions for each activity appear in the text just prior to the activity.
- Begin each session by selecting a volunteer couple to read the introductory poem. Let them decide who will read which portion. Instruct them to read as if they are gifting one another with words and feelings from their own heart and to listen with an open heart to receive the gift.
- To build group cohesion, encourage different couples to read the introductory verses.

- After reading the poem, group members can share their thoughts, feelings and favorite lines or images. Limit the discussion to three to five minutes depending on group size. Stop while interest is high rather than coax participation.
- Next, read the **Reflection** on Love to the group. Ask for questions or comments. Then go over the directions for the enrichment activity with the group and instruct couples to complete it.
- When it is completed, instruct couples to sign the pledge to follow the convenient maintenance schedule for the activity. Emphasize that the follow up schedule is important. Expecting a single experience to transform a relationship into a lifelong soul mate bond, is like buying a new car, filling the tank and expecting the gas to last a life time. **Please read the section regarding maintenance schedules below.**
- **A**fter the activities and signings are completed, read the **Afterthought** to the group. Ask for questions or comments and encourage couples to share what they liked or learned from the session.
- At the beginning **and** end of each session, the group leader gives a gentle reminder that accepting and exercising responsibility for the relationship imparts the power to change and control it. Therefore, how much effort a couple puts into a session **and the follow up activity**, determines how much enrichment they will experience and how soon they will achieve the love centered life described on page 104.
- When the directions instruct couples to set a future date to complete a task, simply proceed with the part of the activity that can be completed during the session.

THE IMPORTANCE OF MAINTENANCE SCHEDULES

Doing an activity once produces a temporary positive effect, but this transient experience is not the true miracle available to you. The convenient maintenance schedule on page xiii is designed to motivate and keep you focused on the positive effects of the activities until they become self-reinforcing habits. **That's when the miracle happens.** Love will become the stabilizing force in your life and keep you living in the moment of love that remains untarnished by events and undiminished by time.

DOUBLE YOUR ENRICHMENT

We recommend completing the enrichment activities within the space provided in this manual and preserve it as a keepsake – a historical document that marks the beginning of your journey to lifelong soul mate love. We also recommend that you preserve all the loving mementoes you create such as photographs, love notes and keepsakes in a nicely decorated box labeled ***Midnight Harvest Treasure Chest – Our Journey to Soul mate Love***.   Add more mementos as you follow the prescribed maintenance schedule after the workshop and book are completed.

CONSTRUCTING YOUR TREASURE CHEST

For individual couples:

- Select a box (a shoe box can be a great starter treasure chest).
- Gather some craft supplies.
- Set aside some time and work together to create a box worthy of holding your romantic mementos.

For groups:
- The group leader can organize an *assembly party* for couples to construct their Treasure Chests either prior to or after the first session. This is an excellent way for couples to get to know each other and build group support.

USING YOUR TREASURE CHEST

 When your heart wants or needs a *touch of love*, a trip through the *collection of mementos* will rejuvenate and strengthen your love bond. Furthermore, saving the mementos and adding new ones in the future will be an experiential record you can share with your family.

These mementos should be shared with children just like a wedding album. Many couples have reported that as part of their anniversary celebration they share the contents of their Treasure Chest with the entire family. Without exception these couples have confirmed that their children are fascinated to learn how love developed between their parents. The new additions each year teaches them that love continues to play a central role in family life and that love is a lifelong commitment. We don't know of a more effective way for passing loving habits to the next generation.

YOUR LIFETIME WARRANTY

All of the activities in our program are based on the basic principles of behavioral and cognitive psychology which have a clinically proven success rate of 80-95%. They are effective and the data from neuroscience indicates that these principles will stand firm and play a key role in the psychology of the twenty-first century.

Thus we say with confidence that, practiced as prescribed in the convenient Maintenance Schedule on the opposite page, these activities will keep your life love centered as described on page 104. Love will become the stabilizing force in your life and keep you living in the moment of love that remains untarnished by events and undiminished by time.

The loving dialogues that begin each activity are adopted from ***Midnight Harvest: Living in the Moment of Love.*** The afterthoughts with annotated insights are adopted from ***Wisdom to Live By.*** The seed activities in sessions 13 and 18 are adopted from *Seeds of Love®* and *Spiritual Seeds of Love®*. (See page 109)

Maintenance Schedule for Soul Mate Relationships

	Daily	Weekly	Monthly	Every 3 mo	Every 6 mo	Annually	As needed
Creating & Harvesting Love	X						
Filling the Reservoir of Love	X						
Litany of Appreciation	X						
Silent Love	X						
Ode to Love	X						
Outshining the Sun		X					
Planting Seeds of Love		X					
Spiritual Seeds of Love		X					
Exploring Spiritual Love			X				
Entering the Cathedral of Love			X				
Opening Love's Door			X				
Romantic Spiritual Imagery			X				
Setting the Course to Soul Mate Love				X			
Legacy of Love				X			
Nature Walk				X			
Affirmation Date					X		
Personalizing Love					X		
Eliminating Negativity							X
Flexible Perspective							X
Forgiveness and Restitution							X
Time Line of Love						X	
Love's Photo Moments						X	

SESSION ONE (Gaining the Power)

Instructions:

For individual couples:

- For maximum effectiveness, please review the general guidelines in the introduction prior to the session.
- Decide who will read the titled portion of the introductory poem and who will read the reply. Read as if you are gifting each other with words found in your own heart.
- Next, share your favorite lines, images, thoughts and feelings about the poem.
- Read the **Reflection**. Exchange related thoughts, especially on the connection between accepting responsibility for your relationship and gaining the power to control it.
- Work through the exercises until you have crafted a joint certificate of ownership.

For groups:

- For maximum effectiveness, please read through the entire session and review the general guidelines in the introduction prior to beginning the session.
- Select a volunteer couple to read the introductory poem. Let the couple decide who will read the opening verse and who will read the reply. After the reading, ask several volunteers to share their favorite lines, images, thoughts and feelings about the poem.
- Read the **Reflection** to the group. Have a discussion on the interconnectedness between accepting responsibility for your relationship and gaining the power to control it. Then proceed with the activity. Instruct couples to work independently or together as indicated.
- As a prelude to the **Certificate of Ownership**, it is helpful to have the group brainstorm ideas for words and images they might want to use for completing their certificate. Then proceed with the activity.
- After part one is completed, have a few couples share what they have drafted. Then instruct couples to work on their **Certificate of Joint Ownership**. As a warm up, it can be helpful to have participants share some of the areas that end up taking priority over their relationship.
- After the **Certificate of Joint Ownership** is completed, ask volunteers to share their work.

Champion of Your Heart

Kiss me only if love fills
Every chamber of your heart
For when our lips touch I shall become your knight
And battle unto death whatever may hinder love's bond.
As your champion
I shall guard your soul with equal valor
So that your love and grace may grow
'Till angels bow in awe of your glory.

Reply

Inflamed with love
I offer my heart to you
My champion
Guard it with vigor and grace
As I shall guard yours.

Reply to Reply

Lady of love and grace
I swear upon the altar of all that is holy
To be your champion
As you shall be mine.
May heaven so bind our souls.

Reflection

About fifty percent of all marriages end in divorce. This means if you simply trust to luck and hope for the best in your relationship, you will have a 50/50 chance of achieving lifelong love. You must accept responsibility and take active steps to ensure that your loving relationship will be the one that will last a lifetime. Wishing and hoping it will last doesn't make it happen. Doing the activities in this manual will!

Please note: **Accepting and exercising the responsibility for something gives us the power to change and control it. The more responsibility we exercise the more control we acquire. Failing to accept the responsibility puts it beyond our power to change or control it.**

Consider this analogy. A new car comes with a Warranty and Maintenance Schedule. The more responsibly you follow the schedule the longer it will last. Accept no responsibility and the car will deteriorate and lose its value. As it loses value you will lose interest in it and begin to think of trading it in. The same process occurs with your marriage. If you don't nurture and care for it, chances are you will lose interest in preserving it and separation or divorce will become a more and more viable option. **Champion of Your Heart** captures the concept of ownership and responsibility in romantic imagery.

Enrichment Activity: Ownership and Responsibility

First you must take ownership of your marital relationship which means that you take responsibility for nurturing its development. In order to do this you need to know what kind of maintenance it requires and how to administer it. The activities in this manual and the maintenance schedule are designed to fulfill these requirements. However you must be ready to accept the responsibility to complete all the sessions and follow the maintenance schedule.

Are you ready to take these steps? Do you want to be in charge of and responsible for turning your marriage into a lifelong series of romantic soul mate adventures? Are you willing to work to integrate the staying power and stability of your spiritual beliefs with your romantic loving experiences to form a soul mate bond?

Circle your answer

YES   NO

Those who chose NO can give this manual to a friend. Those who chose **YES** can proceed to the first activity.

Crafting a Certificate of Ownership

Write a statement of ownership in the box on the opposite page that reflects your determination to shape and control your relationship. Make it as creative, romantic and emphatic as you wish. To help you get started, perform the following activities:

- List three things in nature which are very strong.

_____

- Write three words or phrases that capture the determination you feel for preserving your relationship._____

- Write three words or phrases that capture the essence of love and romance for you.

_____

Now you're ready to craft your statement of ownership. Use some of the words or images you just listed to construct a statement which reflects your determination to build the relationship you want. The following is an example of one spouse's pledge:

> *I, **Mary K.** with all my heart and mind and soul take full responsibility for my marital relationship. I will combine the powers of my mind and soul and the passion of my heart to form a deeply loving, passionate, romantic and soul mate relationship with my spouse whom I love as dearly as life itself. I shall pursue this goal with every breath I take.*

Now let your creative juices flow and write your own pledge in the box below. It's OK to borrow words, phrases, or ideas from the sample. However, you must personalize it with lots of your own words so you feel you are speaking from **your** heart.

Certificate of Ownership

_____

_____

_____

_____

_____

_____

_____

When you are finished, reread your statement to yourself and contemplate the awesome responsibility you just agreed to accept. Then repeat three times: ***"This is what I want to do! This is what I will do!"*** Enjoy the power of your determination!

Now experience one of the wonderful benefits of committed love by doubling your power. Sit facing your spouse, trade books and share what you have just written. After both of you have read each other's **Certificate of Ownership**, agree that you will now share ownership, and maintenance responsibilities. Focus on the good feeling of having a committed partner to help you and enjoy the added confidence, motivation and love as it flows between you.

You are now ready to compose a **Certificate of Joint Ownership** for the relationship **with** a priority statement as in the sample below. Before you begin have a discussion with your spouse and decide what three things tend to take priority over the relationship. This may be uncomfortable to acknowledge, but honesty is a must! Ask each other, "What are the three things that tend to occupy most of your free time?" Work related activity (spilling over into your personal time), sports and shopping are the most common. List them here:

1._____ 2._____ 3._____

Now you are ready to make and sign your joint pledge in the box on the next page in both books.

Guidelines for completing this pledge

Use the results from the earlier exercise by taking parts from each of your individual **Certificates of Ownership** to create the **Certificate of Joint Ownership**. Be sure to list three things that tend to take priority over the relationship as in the sample below.

We, **Mary** and **Marvin,** take mutual responsibility for our loving relationship
and promise to make it our #1 priority more important than
sports, shopping or money; and do the activities learned in this
program on the prescribed basis to achieve a lifelong, happy, and
intensely romantic loving soul mate relationship, courting each other's
soul along with the heart. We take this oath freely without
reservation or hidden agenda and will share the highlights of our
journey to soul mate love with our children.

Now, write your own joint pledge in the box provided below. It's OK to borrow words, phrases, or ideas from the sample. However, make sure you personalize it with your own words, thoughts and feelings so it comes from **your hearts**.

Certificate of Joint Ownership

_____

_____

_____

_____

_____

_____

_____

_____

_____

_____

Signed _____ **and** _____

You are now the champion of each other's heart and soul. Discuss with your spouse what it feels like to be in charge of and responsible for turning your marriage into a very happy, romantic, loving, and lifelong adventure to soul mate love.

Afterthought

When we purchase a new car, the warranty requires that certain minimum maintenance be performed. Yet when it comes to what should be our most treasured possession, our marital relationship, no one gives us a manual or maintenance schedule. The rest of this book will correct that oversight.

Remember, with ownership comes responsibility. With responsibility comes the power to control and change. The activities in this manual will help you to acquire and apply that power.

SESSION TWO (Creating & *Harvesting Love*)

For individual couples: [1]

- For maximum effectiveness please review the general guidelines in the introduction prior to the session.
- Decide who will read the titled portion of the introductory poem and who will read the reply. Read as if you are gifting each other with words found in your own heart.
- After the reading, share your favorite lines, images, thoughts and feelings about the poem.
- Read the **Reflection** and exchange any related thoughts or ideas you wish to share.
- Work independently or together as indicated on the activities that follow. Be sure to sign the pledge at the end of the session.

For groups:

- For maximum effectiveness, please read through the entire session and review the general guidelines in the introduction prior to beginning the session.
- Select a volunteer couple to read the introductory poem. Let the couple decide who will read the opening verse and who will read the reply. After the reading, ask several volunteers to share their favorite lines, images, thoughts and feelings about the poem.
- Read the Reflection to the group. Then have a short, open, group discussion about things spouses love about one another.
- **Then**, instruct spouses to work separately on the *"two things I love most about you"* list**.**
- Next, let several volunteers share what they have written.
- Direct couples to sit quietly for a few moments, hold hands and enjoy the love they have just created and shared with one another.
- Emphasize the importance of following the suggested maintenance schedule.

---

[1] The instructions for couples will remain the same for all subsequent sessions and will not be reprinted.

Harvesting Love

As we sow, we shall harvest
The seeds we plant in each other's heart
Words that blossom into love
Making us see one another
With the freshness of dawn
Searching for new ways to love.

Reply
In every harvest
Each blossom shall render new seeds
Shaping the course of love
Melding heart to soul
Erasing the barrier between time and eternity.

Reflection

As champion of each other's heart and soul you are ready to take the next step of nourishing and fostering the growth of your relationship. As the poem implies, you reap what you sow because each harvest provides the seeds for the next sowing.

Translation: The more effort you put into creating, giving and receiving love, the more love each successive harvest will bring.

Relationships are nourished by love. The more love you create or bring into the relationship, the stronger and healthier it becomes. The beauty of love is that you can create love any time you want. The more love you create, the more love you can give to each other. The more love you exchange, the stronger your bond becomes. **This process of creating and sharing loving thoughts, feelings and experiences is the key to preserving, controlling and increasing the depth and intensity of a loving relationship.**

Enrichment Activity: Let There Be Love

The easiest way to create love is to think about love. In the space provided, list the two things you love most about your spouse. Sit quietly for a few moments and contemplate the happy and loving feelings these qualities generate in you.

Two things I Love about_____

1._____

2._____

 You have just created a moment of love that didn't exist before. Simply by thinking kind, loving thoughts about your spouse, you created loving feelings in yourself. In doing so, you increased your capacity to give love because you are now free to share these loving feelings. Accept and enjoy the power to create love in yourself that the two of you can share. Use this power every day.

 Now, it's time to exercise your increased capacity to give love. Give some moments of joy, satisfaction and love to each other by sharing what you wrote. **Please note: As your spouse reads listen without judgment or self-criticism.** Focus on and accept the positive, loving feelings you experience as you hear what your spouse loves about you. Then switch roles. After each partner has shared, hold hands and discuss what these moments of giving and receiving love felt like and meant. Then write a few notes about the experience in the box below.

_____

_____

_____

You have both increased your capacity to give and receive love, and have strengthened the bond between you. The more often you share loving thoughts or feelings, the stronger your bond of love becomes and the more your relationship becomes love centered.

Now sign the pledge below in both books.

We agree to create and share more moments of love in our daily lives.

Signed _____ and _____

Afterthought

As we say in *Wisdom to Live By*:

> **"Life is a series of moments, each an opportunity to shape those yet to come. The love**
> **you bring into one moment flows into and shapes the next, making**
> **your relationship more love centered."**

The next sessions will focus on methods for creating more love to increase your capacity to give and receive love.

SESSION THREE (*Outshine the Sun*)

For groups:

- For maximum effectiveness, please read through the entire session and review the general guidelines in the introduction prior to beginning the session.
- Select a volunteer couple to read the introductory poem. Let the couple decide who will read the opening verse and who will read the reply. After the reading, ask several volunteers to share their favorite lines, images, thoughts and feelings about the poem.
- Discuss the connection between thoughts and feelings as covered in the reflection.
- Preview the steps for the enrichment activity with the group. Then instruct couples to complete the list.
- After couples have completed their lists, instruct them to share with one another. Be sure to emphasize the cautionary note about the size of the list.
- Next ask for volunteers to share a few things they were pleased to have heard about themselves.
- Emphasize the importance of pursuing this activity as suggested in the maintenance schedule.

OVERLOAD

Thoughts of you arise in my mind
So sweet, so fast
I cannot hold them all.
Faster yet, they come
Like star dust filling the heavens
'Til night outshines the sun.

Reply
Your words
Feed the fire within
Melting the armor that
Protected my heart
Waiting for love.

Reflection

Thought is the most powerful tool couples can use to nurture their relationship. Thoughts generate feelings. Feelings initiate action. Applying this to love means the more often you think loving thoughts, the more often you will have loving feelings. The more loving feelings you have, the more likely you will behave in a sweet and loving manner. That's the message of the poem, and the secret for keeping the flames of love growing **"until night outshines the sun."**

Enrichment Activity: Outshine the Sun

In the space provided below, make a list of **everything** that you like about your spouse. In the previous activity you listed only your top two favorites. Now include everything. Make the list as long as possible. Be sure to include physical traits, personality traits and behavioral mannerisms (For example; smiling often, taking good care of the kids, etc.). Pay attention to your feelings as you make the list.

Things I like about_____

When you are finished, read the list again and say out loud to yourself, **"How lucky I am to have such a wonderful spouse."**

After both of you complete your lists, share them with each other, but **one important cautionary note should be considered.** If you are giving your spouse a very short list, make a commitment to pay more attention and discover more things you like about your spouse. If this proves to be difficult, your expectations are probably too high. Regardless, don't berate yourself. Simply promise your spouse you will work to become more positive in your observations.

If you received a very short list, accept your spouse's promise to change and discuss how both of you can insure those efforts will be successful. Express gratitude that your spouse is willing to work on the problem. **Remember,** this is a program to enrich your relationship, **not** a contest for the Best Spouse Award. With this in mind both spouses should sign the pledge below in both books.

> **We promise to continue to find things we like about each other and to review or add to our list once a week.**
>
> **Signed** _____ **and** _____

Afterthought

Creating love is as easy as thinking. And thinking about things you like about each other serves as springboards for many loving thoughts and feelings. Every time you think of something you like, you generate more love for your **Reservoir of Love** which will be the focus of the next session.

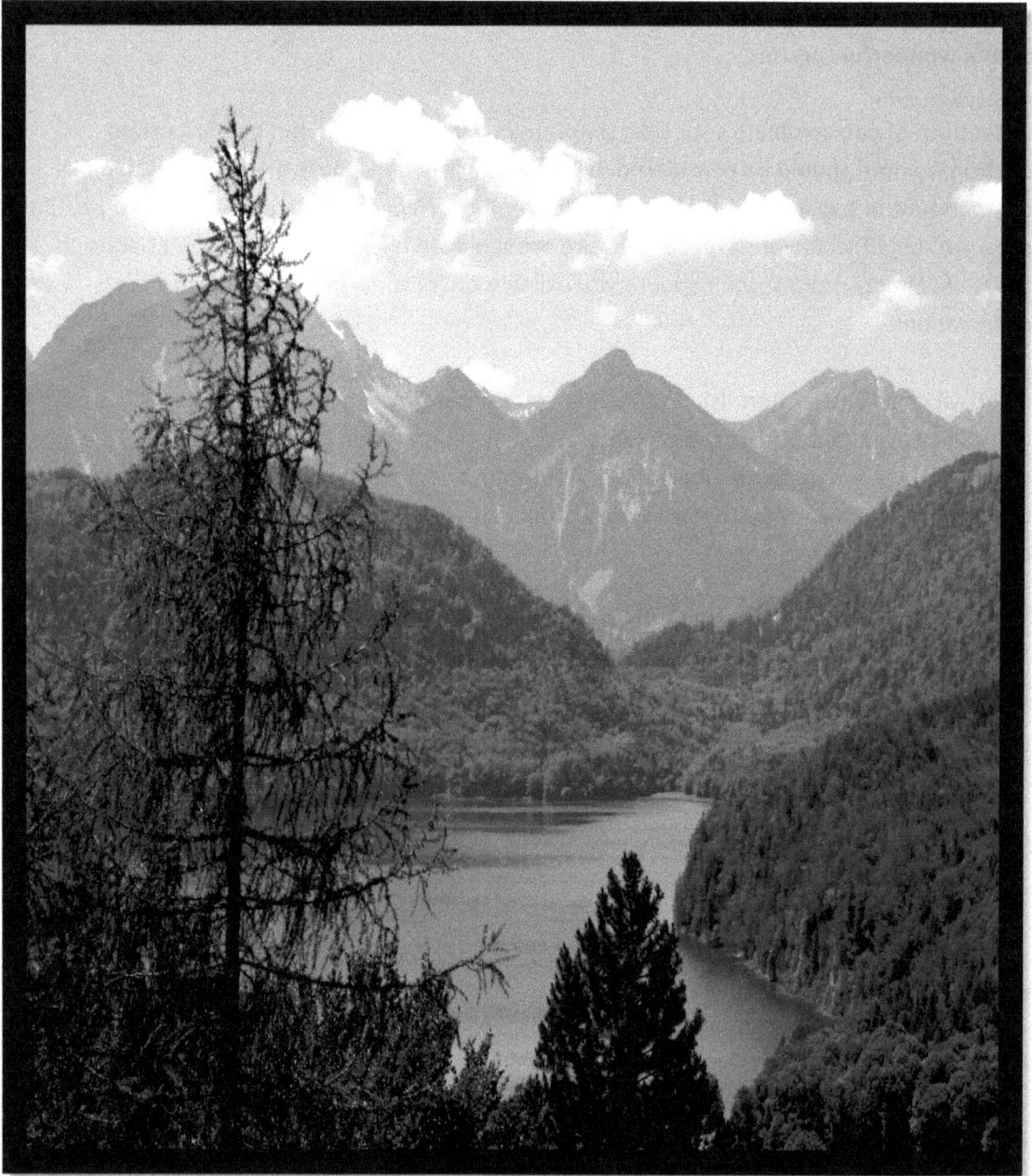

Reservoir of Love   **Photo by Frank Hajcak**
View from Neuschwanstein Castle- Bavaria, Germany

SESSION FOUR (Reservoir of Love)

For groups:

- For maximum effectiveness, please read through the entire session and review the general guidelines in the introduction prior to beginning the session.
- Select a volunteer couple to read the introductory poem. Let the couple decide who will read the opening verse and who will read the reply. After the reading, ask several volunteers to share their favorite lines, images, thoughts and feelings about the poem.
- Discuss the elements of the **Cycle of Love** as covered in the **Reflection**.
- Have an open group discussion about special places that couples holds dear and places that capture romance.
- Encourage couples to create a unique imaginary love haven for their **Reservoir of Love**.
- Finish by having them list four things they will do to start filling their reservoir.
- Emphasize the importance of pursuing this activity according to the suggested maintenance schedule.

Cycle of Love

The gifts you brought into my life
The light of joy
Warmth of love
Peace of soul.
What can I offer in return?

Reply
The gifts we give are the gifts we receive,
Receive from me the kiss that binds the soul.

Reflection

As we previously stated, when you create loving thoughts and feelings in yourself, you automatically increase your capacity to give love because you have more loving feelings you can share with your spouse. Sharing these loving feelings will trigger the **Cycle of Love,** which works like this.

Say you are having affectionate feelings for your spouse and you decide to share them. Your spouse will automatically experience loving feelings toward you, which will trigger a positive reaction such as a smile, a kind word, a loving tender glance or touch. This positive reaction from your spouse will generate more pleasant loving feelings in you, in addition to the ones you already had. Both of you will feel connected and loved as you acknowledge and accept each other's gift of affection. The bonus is the cycle of love may repeat itself.

The deeper or more intense the feelings that you share, the **more often** the cycle of love will repeat itself. Each time the cycle is reactivated both of you gain some loving feelings which did not exist before. The love each of you gains flows into your **Reservoir of Love** which will help you get though any cloudy weather that may come your way.

All this happens because love is a reciprocating, self-reinforcing act. It blesses those who give and those who receive. The giver becomes the receiver and the receiver becomes the giver, every time the cycle completes or repeats itself. Now it's time to build your **Reservoir of Love.**

Enrichment Activity: Reservoir of Love

Just as the body needs a minimum daily requirement of vitamins and minerals to keep healthy, the heart and soul need a minimum daily requirement of love to develop and preserve the soul mate bond. Think of the **Reservoir of Love** as an accumulation of all the surplus love which you and your spouse created and shared that exceeds your minimum daily requirement. This reserve of love will keep your relationship flourishing even in the cloudiest weather.

Constructing, filling and preserving your **Reservoir of Love** is analogous to saving money for a rainy day. Begin saving by creating a private imaginary hide-a-way for your reservoir. This is a place where you can go to re-energize your relationship or add more love to the reservoir.

Discuss with your spouse what kind of hide-a-way will work for both of you. A special spot in the city? In the mountains? On a cloud? In a cave? A secret room in your home? Do you want a fountain? A river? A spring? A lake? Be creative! Decide what you would like now! In the box below, write a brief description of your hide-a-way. Then make a commitment to find a picture or painting that both of you feel represents your private hideaway for storing love. The photo on page 14 is one example of the thousands of possibilities.

_____

_____

_____

_____

Now it's time to begin stocking your reservoir. Working together list four things in the box below that either of you can do to start and keep love flowing into your reservoir. Then, sign the pledge in both books to affirm that you will add to your reservoir with daily thoughts and acts of love. Some examples of things you can do to fill your **Reservoir of Love** might include:

- A heartwarming smile or an affectionate touch.
- You do a chore which your spouse normally does.
- Provide an impromptu neck massage.
- Buy or make your spouse lunch and put a special note in it.

Daily acts of love we will do to keep our Reservoir of Love filled:

1. _____

2. _____

3. _____

4. _____

Signed _____ **and** _____

Building a large reservoir helps to stabilize your relationship and your life. Couples with a large reservoir recover from misfortune faster, survive tragedy better and have happier more romantic relationships. The next sessions will focus on activities that will insure that you have a continuous flow of love into your reservoir.

Afterthought

Some couples keep a pencil, a pad of paper and a small box labeled **OUR RESERVOIR OF LOVE** by the picture that represents their hideaway. The spouse who has a special loving thought or receives an act of affection jots it on a slip of paper and deposits it in the reservoir box. When either or both of you desire a touch of love, read the notes in the reservoir box. Reminiscing about these loving events will energize the **cycle of love**, strengthen your bond and add more love to the reservoir.

As we say in *Wisdom to Live By:*

Failure to plan for tomorrow is like walking backwards into the future.

SESSION FIVE (Nature Walk)

For groups:

- For maximum effectiveness, please read through the entire session and review the general guidelines in the introduction prior to beginning the session.
- Select a volunteer couple to read the introductory poem. Let the couple decide who will read the opening verse and who will read the reply. After the reading, ask several volunteers to share their favorite lines, images, thoughts and feelings about the poem.
- Read the Reflection to the group. Discuss seeing love reflected in the beauty and intricacies of the natural world and how that will create more opportunities to think about love and generate more loving feelings.
- Emphasize the importance of pursuing this activity according to the suggested maintenance schedule.

Silent Song of Love

The soft flutter of butterfly wings
The delicate flight of the dandelion seed
The morning glory opening to greet the sun
Resplendent lilacs swaying in the warm spring breeze
My voice joins each silent note in praise of you.

Reply

I sense your song in the silent
Ebb and flow of life around me
My heart rejoices in each note
And bids my tongue join the chorus
In gratitude for you.

Reflection

The natural rhythms of nature such as day and night, the changing seasons, the blooming and withering of flowers and life itself are all excellent sources for reflecting on love. Learning to see love in all that surrounds us creates a feeling of connectedness to **the grand design of creation,**

The Road through the Aspen and Pines   Watercolor by Julie Vollmer ©2010

the source of all love. Tapping into this wealth of nature allows you to experience new dimensions and intensities of love.

Enrichment Activity: Nature Walk

Think of some of your favorite natural images that symbolize love. Some examples might be a rose, a sunset, or a moonlit night. Nature is an excellent source of romantic inspiration which can be used to strengthen your relationship. In this activity, you will make a direct connection between love and nature, share it with your spouse and strengthen your bond of love.

Independent of your spouse, go on a nature walk in a garden, a park or the woods. Find something natural (a leaf, a branch, a flower, a bud, etc.) that you feel captures, symbolizes or reflects your love for your spouse. Give your selection to your spouse and explain how it reflects or represents your love. **Next** write the explanation in the space below. Be sure to store the objects given to each other in your **"Midnight Harvest Treasure Chest".**

The Symbol of my Love for you is_____**. It reminds me of my love for you**

because_____.

Afterthought

Giving your spouse a symbol from nature along with words of love has a greater impact and longer shelf life than words alone. Nature is an abundant source of intricate, lovely things that can easily be related to love. We recommend **a Nature Walk** once every season. We have yet to meet a couple that doesn't enjoy this activity. Decide what's right for you, fill in the box below in both books and set a date for your next one here _____/_____/_____.

We will plan a Nature walk at least once every

_____

Signed _____ **and** _____

SESSION SIX (Personalizing Love)

For groups:

- For maximum effectiveness, please review the general guidelines prior to the session.
- Have a volunteer couple read the introductory poem. Let them decide who will read the opening verse and who will read the reply. After the reading, ask for several volunteers to share their favorite lines or images and thoughts and feelings about them.
- Discuss the importance of anchoring and seeing love everywhere as covered in the Reflection.
- Instruct couples to complete the exercise by filling in the blanks, and sharing the results with their spouse.
- Ask volunteers to share their favorites with the group.

Transformation

As the rising sun transforms the earth
From grey shadow to vivid color
Your love transforms my life.
Notes become symphonies
Words-poems
Threads-tapestries.
Life became art.

Reply

Your love revealed secrets
Unlocked my heart
Released my soul.
Everything I see, hear, touch and feel
Is so much more.
We are the symphony
The poem
The tapestry.
Love became Art.

Reflection

Love is infinite and everywhere. We just have to learn to see it. For example, say you expand your concept of love to include flowers and stars. Then any time you see either, you will have thoughts of love, which can be shared or stored in your reservoir of love. This process, of creating associations to form a relationship between two entities is called **anchoring**.

 The more anchors for love a couple creates, the more opportunities they will have for loving thoughts or interactions. The fewer anchors a couple has, the less often thoughts of love will enter their minds. So tap into this cycle by expanding your vision of what love is and then personalizing it in the activity below.

Enrichment Activity: Expanding and Personalizing Love

Work independently and use the box provided below. Complete the six sentences. The object is to produce six different responses without regard to logic or correctness. Fantasy and humor are fine. **There are no wrong answers.**

> Examples: Love is like **the moon** because **it lights up the night**!
> Love is like **a circle** because **it never ends**!
> Love is like **a house** because **it feels warm and safe!**

1. Love is like _____ because_____.

2. Love is like _____ because _____.

3. Love is like _____ because _____.

4. Love is like _____ because _____.

5. Love is like _____ because _____.

6. Love is like _____ because _____.

Next, pick the three you like the best and personalize the analogy. Begin each with the words: **My love for you**, as in the following example.

<u>My love for you</u> is like <u>a circle</u> because <u>it will never end</u>.

1.	_____	is like_____	because _____
2.	_____	is like_____	because _____
3.	_____	is like_____	because _____

When both of you are finished, present the personalized analogies to each other verbally. Laughter, hugs and kisses are part of the fun. Enjoy each other's reaction.

Congratulations!   You have just taken the first step toward releasing your inner romantic poet! You take another step every time you personalize an analogy about love. Take as many steps as you wish as often as you desire.

We suggest doing this activity at least twice a year simply because the more ways you think about love the more doors you open for loving thoughts and interactions to enter your relationship. As you will see in session 13 your, "**My love for you,**" statements can be used as a *Seed of Love*. ® Now in both books, sign the pledge below and set a date for your next personalization session here_____/_____/_____.

We agree to have fun personalizing love twice a year.
Signed_____ and _____

Afterthought

The poem tells us that **Love is art and art is everywhere.** The more love you bring into each day, the more beautiful a masterpiece you create.

SESSION SEVEN (Affirmation Date)

For groups:

- For maximum effectiveness, please read through the entire session and review the general guidelines in the introduction prior to beginning the session.
- Select a volunteer couple to read the introductory poem. Let the couple decide who will read the opening verse and who will read the reply. After the reading, ask several volunteers to share their favorite lines, images, thoughts and feelings about the poem.
- Reinforce how important it is for couples to express their appreciation, admiration and respect to one another and remind them that no one knows how another person feels unless that person tells them.
- Instruct couples to complete the affirmations, transfer them to 3x5 cards (which you will provide) and select a date on which the affirmations will be shared. **Do not share them now.**
- Remind them to write a quick statement about their reaction to the shared affirmations after it is completed.
- Emphasize the importance of following the suggested maintenance schedule and to record any new material on 3x5 cards to store in their **Midnight Harvest Treasure Chest**.

Ode to Our Love

May the sun of long life shine upon you,
My love surround you,
And the light of joy guide you
Through the darkness that may befall you.
May you find the beauty I see within you
Before your soul decides to leave you.
May choirs of angels be there to greet you
With the love I failed to give you,
The peace that overlooked you
And the joy that passed by you
When your soul decides to leave you.

Reply

May the sun of long life shine upon us,
The love we share surround us
And the light of joy be there to guide us
Through the darkness that may befall us.
May we find the beauty within us
Before our souls decide to leave us.

Reflection

Committed soul mate love is like a delicate flower. It needs to be watered every day with gentleness, kindness, joy, passion and most of all recognition and appreciation. Recognition and appreciation are the primary nutrients which make the flower grow healthy and strong. Give it plenty of both and reap a big harvest.

Unfortunately spouses often put off or forget to tell each other exactly what they like, respect and appreciate about each other. Sometimes we falsely assume they already know how we feel. The poem emphasizes the importance of doing it now.

Enrichment Activity: An Affirmation Date

Set a date for a night out with your spouse. Write the date on the line in the **Highlights of Our Date** box on the next page.

Next, working separately, prepare a set of **Affirmations** that you will present to your spouse when you are on the date. Complete the Affirmations on the lines below. Copy them onto 3x5 index cards to facilitate the sharing on your date. **Do not share these cards now!**

Three things that attracted me to you in the beginning of our relationship:

1. _____

2. _____

3. _____

Three moments/ memories during the course of our relationship that are very special to me:

1. _____

2. _____

3. _____

Three things I admire about you now:

1. _____

2. _____

3. _____

After the exchange is completed, share your reaction to giving and receiving the Affirmations. Write a quick note that highlights your reaction in the box below. Be sure to store the 3x5 cards in your *Midnight Harvest Treasure Chest*.

Highlights of Our Date on _____

_____

_____

_____

_____

_____

Discuss how frequently you and your spouse would enjoy an affirmation date. (We highly recommend a minimum of twice a year.) Fill in the box below in both books.

We agree to have an Affirmation Date every ___ months.

Signed_____ and _____

Afterthought

Affirmations that are exchanged between spouses are a great way to build each other's self confidence and self esteem. This is also an easy and enjoyable way to add to your **Reservoir of Love**. On future **Affirmation Dates,** both of you should focus on what you admire about each other now **and** a recent moment that was special since the last **Affirmation Date**.

SESSION EIGHT (Love's Photo Moment)

For groups:

- For maximum effectiveness, please read through the entire session and review the general guidelines in the introduction prior to beginning the session.
- Select a volunteer couple to read the introductory poem. Let the couple decide who will read the opening verse and who will read the reply. After the reading, ask several volunteers to share their favorite lines, images, thoughts and feelings about the poem.
- Discuss the importance of sharing favorite memories related to their relationship and encourage several volunteers to provide examples.
- Instruct couples to work independently of each other to take photos of places that played an important role in the development of their love and bring them to the next session to share with the group.
- Complete this activity as far as the instructions suggest.
- When participants bring in photos, allow everyone to share photos and to discuss what they wrote in their handbooks.
- Emphasize the importance of pursuing this activity according to the suggested maintenance schedule and storing the photos in their *Midnight Harvest Treasure Chest*.

Connecting

Memories of us standing in the shadow of love's door
Forming images that one by one make their home in our hearts,
Gently cleansing our souls like warm spring rains,
Connecting two dreams, two hearts, two souls.

Reply

Your spirit moves through me
Like thread through the eye of a needle
We weave a tapestry of love.

Reflection

A mutually appreciative, committed lifelong relationship is the greatest earthly joy two people can share. All those special memories of the past, the potential of the present and all the hopes for the future create a pool of joy that strengthens the love bond. Sharing and reminiscing together is a powerful tool that will help you through the more difficult times. Reflecting on these memories captures the beauty of the relationship and its potential, and keeps you focused on your goal of lifelong bonding. Photos are an excellent way to capture and preserve these magical moments.

Enrichment Activity: Photo Moment

Working independently, each spouse will take a picture of two different places that played an important role in the development of your relationship. If this is not possible because you have relocated to a new city and don't have a photo scrapbook, take photos of places or things that are important to your relationship now. (A hillside, a park bench, backyard, fireplace, the restaurant of your first date, or where you first realized the two of you were in love.)

On the back of each photo you select, write the following information.

This is a picture of_____.

It's important to me because this is where _____.

When the photos are ready, set a date for a romantic evening out. Spouses are to take turns presenting the photos to each other and explaining in detail why it is important. Share thoughts and feelings you experienced as you took the photos as well as your reactions to the exchange. Jot a note that highlights your reaction on the back of each photo you received and store the photos in your **Midnight Harvest Treasure Chest**.

Set a target date for completing this project and **write it on this line**____/_____/_____.

Then, discuss the possibility of an annual photo moment that highlights one or two high points of your relationship since your last Photo Date. Many couples use anniversaries or cupid's day for this activity. Fill in the pledge below in both books.

Our Annual Photo Moment will be held on _____.

Signed_____ **and** _____

Afterthought

Photo dates are not photo of the year competitions! Stay focused on the loving memories and the meaning each photo has for the one who took it. Only positive statements are permitted. Acknowledge and accept what your spouse is offering to you which is a wonderful memory that helped formed the loving bond between the two of you.

SESSION NINE (Opening the Door to Love)

For groups:

- For maximum effectiveness, please read through the entire session and review the general guidelines in the introduction prior to beginning the session.
- Select a volunteer couple to read the introductory poem. Let the couple decide who will read the opening verse and who will read the reply. After the reading, ask several volunteers to share their favorite lines, images, thoughts and feelings about the poem.
- Lead a discussion about some misunderstandings which may have resulted from couples trying to read one another's mind. As in session seven, remind them that no one knows what another person thinks or feels unless that person actually tells them.
- Instruct couples to complete the activity, share with each other, and complete their resolutions.
- Encourage several volunteer couples to share some of their resolutions.
- Emphasize the importance of pursuing this activity according to the suggested maintenance schedule.

Without You

My mind lost in a waking dream
Struggles to find its thoughts
Helpless, like a bird clipped of its wings
My voice cannot find its tongue.
Without you, I am
An empty gift box on Christmas morn.

Reply

Your words are precious glass seeds
Sown in my heart
Where they shall grow into diamonds
With infinite facets
Reflecting the love you brought into my life.

Reflection

Sometimes we have trouble expressing affectionate and tender feelings. Perhaps we feel inadequate because we don't know which words to use. We may fear it might sound silly or trite or that our spouse may not appreciate it. So, we avoid taking the risk and rationalize our lack of action by saying to ourselves, "My spouse knows how I feel." As we said in session seven the fact is no one knows how you feel until you express it.

There are a million ways to say "I love you," and no one ever tires of hearing they are loved. Open the door to better communication by letting your spouse know you have the desire to express tender feelings openly and honestly. Work to discover what is blocking the ability to express love. Challenge yourselves to keep the door to communication open in order to facilitate the flow of loving feelings and words.

Enrichment Activity: Opening the Door to Love

Work independently to complete these sentences:

a) I'd like to be able to share my loving and affectionate feelings openly with you. When I try to express these feelings I sometimes feel:

_____

_____

b) In order to share my feelings openly with you, I need:

_____

_____

c) To encourage more mutual exchanges of loving thoughts and feelings I think we need:

_____

_____

After 5-10 minutes, take turns sharing responses with one another using the following guidelines:

- There can be no criticism or negative judgments.
- During the sharing, the speaker is not to be interrupted.
- Resist the urge to finish your spouse's sentences or correct your spouse if you disagree.
- One spouse begins by sharing what was written for sentence (**a**) in the previous exercise.
- The other listens with the heart and restates what was heard.
- Accept what your spouse tells you at face value. This is not a debate or contest to determine who is right or wrong. The idea is to learn what blocks the expression of tender feelings from both of your perspectives.
- When both of you feel you understand what the block may be, move onto sentence (**b**) of the same exercise. Make sure each of you has a clear idea of what the other needs.
- Proceed to sentence (**c**) and share the ideas each of you have written.

The last part of this activity requires you and your spouse to agree on three things that will be done to over-come the noted obstacles and facilitate expressing affectionate thoughts and feelings. For example resolutions could include:

- Agreeing to schedule a time for sharing.
- Agreeing to use a timer to guarantee no one interrupts.
- Establishing a special place to share your expressions.
- Agreeing to exchange tender feelings even if you feel awkward.

Resolutions are sealed with a kiss! Enter your resolutions in the box on the next page. Remember these are three resolutions which both of you are willing to help each other keep. Sign the agreements on the next page, in both books.

We agree that:

1. _____

2. _____

3. _____

Signed_____ **and** _____

Afterthought

It's natural to feel awkward or hesitant when trying something new. It simply means you need more practice. What could be more fun than practicing the ability to create and express tender, affectionate feelings? Expressing these tender feelings is a special way to share the nuances of love and to add to your reservoir.

Schedule time as needed or desired according to what both of you agreed to do. However, it is important to schedule a monthly "quick check" to make sure you are sticking to your resolutions. If you are not, set up a time and date to discuss what needs to be done to get back on track.

We agree to schedule a monthly check up to determine if we are on track with our resolutions.

Signed _____ **and** _____

Untitled   *Watercolor by Julie Vollmer©2006*

SESSION TEN (Eliminate Negativity)

For groups:

- For maximum effectiveness, please read through the entire session and review the general guidelines in the introduction prior to beginning the session.
- Select a volunteer couple to read the introductory poem. Let the couple decide who will read the opening verse and who will read the reply. After the reading, ask several volunteers to share their favorite lines, images, thoughts and feelings about the poem.
- Discuss how negativity interferes with the natural flow of love and crowds out the positive feelings and emotions. Emphasize that the more negativity there is in a relationship, the less room there is for the positive.
- Emphasize the importance of pursuing this activity according to the suggested maintenance schedule.

Winds of Love

Galactic winds of love
Silencing songs of sorrows past
Nursing imperfections,
As buds about to bloom
Prepare our souls for celestial flight.

Reply
You are spirit, I am flesh
We intertwine as wind and branches
Whispering of love breathed into our souls.

Reflection

Tolerance is the cornerstone of a mature relationship. This does not mean tolerating mental or physical abuse. It does mean that couples will accept the thoughts, feelings and idiosyncrasies of each other and have empathy for one another's foibles, difficulties or frustrations. It also means you will not try to change one another to fit your own whims and desires or to mirror your own thoughts and ideas.

The more tolerance spouses develop for each other's differences, the more stable the relationship becomes. Tolerant couples have fewer arguments because they appreciate differences in one another and understand that diversity is strength. They build on each others' strengths and learn to love each other unconditionally more easily.

There are two kinds of tolerance needed to maintain a healthy relationship. One is accepting personal foibles or faults. The other is accepting differences in opinions, preferences and desires. In this session we will work on the former.

Enrichment Activity: Eliminating Negativity

Copy the list of everything you like and admire about your spouse from the third Session. Add any new ones you might have missed. Or, if you prefer, you can make a completely new **Admiration List** in the space below.

Admiration List

_____   _____   _____

_____   _____   _____

_____   _____   _____

_____   _____   _____

_____   _____   _____

_____   _____   _____

_____   _____   _____

_____   _____   _____

_____   _____   _____

On the line below, write the personal foible of your spouse that is most difficult for you to accept.

_____

Please Note:

Which foible of yours do you think your spouse finds most problematic? If you find it difficult to be reminded of one of your foibles, we recommend that you contemplate the definition of *humility* found in *Wisdom to Live By*.

"Humility is realizing what a wonderful person you are and at the same time realizing how much you need to improve."

Now read your **Admiration List** from the above box and focus on the pleasant feelings that arise within you as you appreciate each item. End the reading by saying, "All these wonderful traits far outweigh this one that's a challenge. I'm truly fortunate to have such a wonderful spouse". Repeat these two sentences three times and speak with conviction.

Then repeat this entire procedure a few more times until you are certain you feel a little more tolerant of the foible. Next, copy the positive list on a 3x5 index card. Fold the card and put it in a handy place like your wallet, so you can use it in a couple of different ways.

First it can be used as a counterweight for any negative thoughts about your spouse that may arise during the day. For example, when you have a disagreement before leaving for work, you may start to ruminate and have negative thoughts about your spouse during the day. Instead of allowing yourself to become upset or angry, use your list to stop the negative thoughts and feelings. Here's how.

Every time you find yourself thinking negative thoughts about your spouse just say: "**Stop!**" Then take out your list and read it as above. Sometimes you will need to read it several times to stop the negative thoughts. Do this consistently and eventually your brain will be rewired to automatically short circuit negative ruminations about your spouse as soon as they begin.

This does not mean that you ignore something your spouse maybe doing which is detrimental to you or the relationship. It simply means you should weigh things out and stop focusing on the little nit-picky items that cause most couples to argue.

How can you tell which are the little nit-picky things? Here's one way. Simply ask yourself, "Will this still matter five years from now?" An emphatic, "No!" means it's not worth the energy of ruminating or arguing. Just pull out your list and count your blessings. If you answer "Yes," then ask yourself "What percentage of the population would agree with me." If you cannot honestly believe that at least 75% of the population would agree with you, pull out your list and count your blessings. Truly most things couples argue about fall into the nit-picky range.

The second use for your **Admiration List** is called the **Oyster Method** because just like an oyster you can turn a minor irritation into a pearl of love. The next time you're waiting in a long checkout line, caught in a traffic jam or suffering an airline delay, pull out your list. Instead of getting caught up in the anger and frustration of the situation, enjoy pleasant thoughts about your spouse and add to your **Reservoir of Love**.

Now read and sign the pledge below in both books.

We promise to use the Admiration List as needed to eliminate negative ruminations and to increase the love in our Reservoir.

Signed _____ and _____

Afterthought

Each time you stop negative ruminations about your spouse you open the door for more positive feelings and interactions in your relationship. We strongly recommend using this list consistently and frequently. In the next session we will work on increasing tolerance for differences of opinion, wants and desires.

SESSION ELEVEN (Flexible Perspective)

Gaining a new perspective on arguments

For groups:

- For maximum effectiveness, please read through the entire session and review the general guidelines in the introduction prior to beginning the session.
- Select a volunteer couple to read the introductory poem. Let the couple decide who will read the opening verse and who will read the reply. After the reading, ask several volunteers to share their favorite lines, images, thoughts and feelings about the poem.
- Discuss the origin and nature of arguments as covered in the **Reflection**.
- Clarify the difference between fruitful and unfruitful arguments.
- Discuss how shifting perspectives is not the same as giving up or ignoring your own point of view. Emphasize that a flexible perspective is the earmark of maturity.
- Instruct couples to complete the first part of the exercise and define their issue.
- When everyone has finished, ask a volunteer couple to demonstrate the reverse argument. (Be prepared to demonstrate it yourself).
- After the demonstration, have all couples practice their reverse arguments. Assist those who are having difficulties.
- Before closing, have a short discussion on the virtue of open-mindedness as a deterrent to arguments and have everyone sign the **Attitude Adjustment Pledge** on page 44.
- Emphasize the importance of pursuing this activity according to the suggested maintenance schedule.

Ineffable love

I think of you, speak of you, dream of you
My eyes are blind to all but you.
Gentle fires race across my skin,
Each moment giving rise to yet another tender ache.

In search of relief I chase you from my mind
But the thoughts return a hundred fold,
Forcing your name across my lips
Commanding my heart to open the gates of love.
Still, no words find my tongue.

Reply

Words are but obstacles that stem the flow of love.
The heart knows what the tongue cannot speak
And fills the silence between words with love.
May our words be few.

Reflection

Arguments rarely settle any differences between spouses and often create residual guilt, anger or resentment. These repercussions hinder the natural flow of love. Thus, it's important to keep arguments to a minimum. We can significantly reduce the number of arguments we have or resolve the ones we do have more quickly, if we understand the dynamics behind them.

Some arguments develop because one or both spouses have a narrow or rigid perspective and cannot see the other spouse's point of view. Other arguments begin because one or both spouses fail to express the issue or opinion clearly or present it in an inflammatory manner. Still others surface because one spouse feels the other is ignoring an important issue.

Arguments continue because both spouses believe that only one person is correct, fair and reasonable (**me**). Therefore the other (**you**) must be wrong, unfair or unreasonable. The argument turns from an effort to seek resolution into a contest of who is right and who is wrong.

Enrichment Exercise: Flexible Perspective

First, you and your spouse must agree on an issue that has been a source of friction. Write the issue on the lines below.

_____

_____

Second, independent of each other, fill in the box on the next page and state your opinion or perspective of the issue you agreed to resolve. Take your time. The issue should be stated briefly and clearly. Avoid accusatory phrases like, "You never," or "You always." And no emotionally loaded or inflammatory words like, "That's childish, ridiculous, or dumb," are permitted.

Hint: State the issues in terms of what you want, think, or feel. Begin with an *"I statement"* and be specific. For example: "I would like you to complement me more often." Or, "I think we argue too much about money and I would like us to agree on some basic rules for spending."

The issue for me is:

_____

_____

_____

_____

When you are sure it is written so your spouse will clearly understand your perspective, trade handbooks and read what your spouse has written. At this point some couples may be surprised. Suddenly there is no issue or the problem seems much easier to resolve.

Two primary factors make this work. First, taking time to think through an issue keeps you focused on the problem and helps you to state it clearly. Second, writing it out helps avoid inflammatory or blaming words that fuel new arguments which are far removed from the issue. So if you want to eliminate most of your arguments, simply agree that as soon as your discussion becomes heated or off topic all exchanges must be written. No talking allowed!

 Couples who use this method are often surprised at how few arguments they have and how quickly those they do have get resolved. They rapidly learn that most arguments simply are not worth the time and effort it takes to write them on paper.

If the writing method does not help resolve the issue, let the debate begin. However, there is a twist. Each spouse must defend the other spouse's perspective or statement of the issue. At first, this may feel uncomfortable and perhaps seem impossible, but it can be done.

Hint: Couples having difficulty can pretend they are actors in a play where they have to convince a friend to believe what their spouse wrote. If resolution still cannot be reached, both spouses must sign the agreement in the box on the next page in both books.

> **We agree that we have an irresolvable difference and that it is OK to disagree because we love and respect each other.**
>
> Signed _____ and _____

Extreme difficulty in shifting perspectives means the primary cause of your arguments is an inability to see another person's point of view. Developing a flexible perspective is a prerequisite for resolving conflicts and taking your relationship to the soul mate level. Therefore all couples must read and sign both boxes below in both books.

> **I promise to adopt the attitudes:**
>
> 1) **My opinion is just an opinion, not a fact, and thus can be changed. Therefore neither one of us is right or wrong.**
> 2) **Fairness or reasonableness is simply a matter of exercising my ability to change perspectives. The person who can see the other's point of view is fair and reasonable.**
> 3) **As soon as we lose our focus on the issue or our discussion becomes inflamed and angry, we agree to stop the verbal exchange and switch to the written word.**
>
> Signed _____ and _____

Finally discuss and agree on two specific things you will do to increase tolerance in your relationship. Some examples are:

- Use time out periods when tempers flare.
- Resort to the writing method.
- Ask each other if this will matter 5 years from now.
- Stop and schedule the argument for three days later. In most cases neither spouse will have the desire to continue.

We agree to use the following methods as needed to reduce the number of argument we have.

1._____

2._____

Signed_____ and _____

Afterthought

Now go the extra nine yards. Print the following adage on a 3x5 card in big bold letters and keep it on your desk or refrigerator.

"An opinionated person is one whose opinion can't be swayed by facts. A gullible person is one whose opinion can be swayed without facts. An open minded person is one who looks at the facts to see if a change of opinion is warranted." (From: *Wisdom to Live By.*)

SESSION TWELVE (Restoring the Natural Flow of Love)
Forgiveness and Restitution

For groups:

- For maximum effectiveness, please read through the entire session and review the general guidelines in the introduction prior to beginning the session.
- Select a volunteer couple to read the introductory poem. Let the couple decide who will read the opening verse and who will read the reply. After the reading, ask several volunteers to share their favorite lines, images, thoughts and feelings about the poem.
- Discuss the importance and difficulty of true forgiveness.
- Discuss how crucial restitution is for demonstrating heartfelt sorrow and how it makes granting true forgiveness easier.
- Provide a few examples of hurts or resentments that couples may harbor. (It's best to present minor annoyances.) Then brainstorm as a group and produce some possible types of restitution. Be sure to produce at least three different restitutions for each offense.
- Let couples work on their own hurts or resentments and define the restitution that would work for them.
- Instruct them to work on restitution and forgiveness after the session ends and to sign each others' forgiveness box after restitution is completed and forgiveness is granted.
- Emphasize the importance of pursuing this activity according to the suggested maintenance schedule.
- NOTE: If any couples are stymied, you can instruct them individually on the **Headstone** or the **Monument** methods.

Healing Love

Your soul a pool of absolution
With the healing power of 1000 suns
Unlocks doors that hide wounds we bore
Pain no one can see.
Monuments to old hurts crumble
Making our hearts eager for love.

Reply
The fire that lights the stars
Ignites our hearts
Consuming boundaries
Of day and night, life and death, you and I
Purifying our souls to seek love's destiny.

Reflection

"Unforgiven wounds create their own realties that hide the pain you need to feel and express so that love can heal the wound." *(From: Wisdom to Live By.)*

As the poem and the adage points out, holding grudges, hurts or resentments from the past impedes the natural flow of love because they hide the absence of and hunger for love, which lies beneath them. Thus, it is important to identify and eradicate these blocks and restore the flow of love so that our hearts and souls will be healed and free **"to seek love's destiny."** This is a twofold process; making restitution and granting forgiveness.

 The offended spouse must honestly forgive the offending spouse. The offending spouse must earn the forgiveness by making restitution to the offended spouse. A repentant attitude must be coupled with sincere efforts to assure that the offence will not be repeated.

Enrichment Activity: Forgiveness and Restitution

The **first step** in this process is to acknowledge your hurt or resentment and communicate it to your spouse. Complete the statement below by describing clearly, succinctly and without exaggeration, the hurt or resentment you would like to resolve. For your first restitution-forgiveness experience, it is advisable not to pick a deep, painful issue.

I feel hurt/ resentful because _____

_____

_____

Next write the hurt on a 3x5 card and keep it in your ***Midnight Harvest Treasure Chest.*** You will need it for the burial ceremony.

The **second step** is to decide what restitution you want that would help to heal this hurt or resentment. This requires thoughtful consideration because once restitution is made; you must truly forgive your spouse and consider the matter settled. Be reasonable. It is best if the restitution is related to the offense. For example, the spouse who perpetually forgets birthdays, anniversaries etc. must remember those days in the coming year and create a few new special days to honor the forgiving spouse.

Write the restitution you desire here.

_____

_____

Work on one issue at a time. The spouse who wishes to go first, hands the workbook to the other spouse to read and consider. Then discuss how and when the restitution will be completed. Fill in the box below. Then switch roles and work on the other spouse's issue.

Write what was agreed upon in this box.

_____

_____

When restitution is completed, sign the forgiveness box in the appropriate spouse's book. Write the words, **PAID IN FULL. I AM NO LONGER HURT**, in the box on the next page and on the 3x5 card which you saved. Burn it or burry it. Then kiss and make up. Celebrate the good feeling of having restored the natural flow of love. Repeat the same procedure for the other spouse's hurt or resentment.

```
┌─────────────────────────────────────────────┐
│                                               │
│              Forgiveness Box                  │
│                                               │
│   _____ │
│                                               │
│      Signed_____  │
│                                               │
│                                               │
└─────────────────────────────────────────────┘
```

NOTE: Couples who cannot think of an appropriate restitution or simply can't forgive the offense should complete the **Headstone** or **Monument** method described below.

Headstone Method: In the space provided on the next page draw a headstone for your grave. On the headstone, let the world know how your spouse hurt you or what you resented. For example, your headstone might read, "Here lies (your name). My spouse once called me stupid … said I was a lousy housekeeper … made fun of me in front of my friends etc."

Every day you must read the headstone and accept that this is how you want people to remember you. Picture your family and friends reading it and feeling sorry for you. Repeat daily until you feel ready to forgive your spouse or you can think of an acceptable restitution. Either way, proceed as previously outlined until you kiss and make up.

Monument Method: Draw a monument, like the Lincoln Memorial or Washington Monument, dedicated to your hurt or resentment. Picture thousands of people reading the dedication and feeling sorry for you because your spouse was so insensitive. Repeat daily until you feel ready to forgive your spouse or you can think of an acceptable restitution. Then proceed as previously described until you kiss, and make up.

DRAW A PICTURE OF YOUR HEADSTONE OR A MONUMENT TO YOUR HURT IN THE BOX ON THE NEXT PAGE.

Why it Works

Restitution invites forgiveness because it shows you understand what you did was wrong or unfair and you accept responsibility for what you did. It also indicates that you respect your spouse's feelings and value the relationship enough to repair any damage that may have resulted from your behavior or omission.

Forgiveness shows you acknowledge, accept and respect your spouse's efforts to make amends and that you are ready to relinquish your hurt feelings for the sake of the relationship. In effect, you prove to each other that your relationship is your number one priority.

Now sign the pledge below in both books.

We agree to use the restitution and forgiveness method as needed.

Signed _____ and _____

Afterthought

Contemplate the quote below from *Wisdom to Live By*, print it on a 3x5 card and store it in your **Midnight Harvest Treasure Chest** for future reference.

"Forgiveness through restitution is the only way to restore the natural flow of love because it cleanses guilt from the soul of the offender and cleanses anger, hurt and resentment from the soul of the offended."

SESSION THIRTEEN (Silent Love and Planting Seeds of Love®)

For groups:

- For maximum effectiveness, please read through the entire session and review the general guidelines in the introduction prior to beginning the session.
- Select a volunteer couple to read the introductory poem. Let the couple decide who will read the opening verse and who will read the reply. After the reading, ask several volunteers to share their favorite lines, images, thoughts and feelings about the poem.
- Ask group members to share ideas on how to demonstrate love through actions.
- Have spouses sit across from one another and do the "Silent Love" enrichment activity, share their work, and sign the pledge.
- Discuss the concept of *Seeds* of Love® and instruct couples to create and plant some of their own.
- Ask couples to bring samples to a later session and share some of the fun places they planted the seeds.
- Remind everyone to store the seeds that have been planted and harvested in their **Midnight Harvest Treasure Chest** and of the importance of following the suggested maintenance schedule.

Language of the Heart

Words forming in my heart
A poet's song
Love running deep without a sound
Alas! The tongue knows not the language of the heart.

Reply

Fret not sweet love
The heart feels the eloquence of one loving deed
More than the voices of a hundred poets.

Reflection

We all like to be told that we are loved. But sometimes, "the tongue knows not the language of the heart."   There are 1,000 ways to say "I love you" without speaking a single word. We tend to forget that actions often speak more eloquently than words. Furthermore there are times our partners act in ways that speak of love loudly but we just weren't paying attention.

The poem captures the concept that one kind, loving deed is worth a 100 kind, loving words. One kind deed that is acknowledged also adds oodles of love to your **Reservoir of Love**. That's why it's important to tune into and acknowledge the loving deeds spouses do for each other that are often overlooked or taken for granted.

Enrichment Activity: Silent Love

Couples sit on the floor facing one another. Without saying a word, spouses must let each other know that they love and care for one another. You might try a soft loving touch or a warm smile though there are dozens of possibilities.

Next, working separately, in the box below, list four different wordless ways your spouse can let you know you are loved. Be as creative and romantic as you dare. When you are both finished, silently trade workbooks in a way that adds a touch of love or romance.

My dear sweet, loving_____:

I know I love you dearly and I trust you love me too. Here are some wordless ways you can express your love to me.

1. _____

2. _____

3. _____

4. _____

Discuss the option of having a wordless love exchange once a day. Sign the pledge on the next page, return the handbook to your spouse and sign the pledge in your book too. Committing to a daily exchange of wordless love may seem artificial, but it will quickly become a natural part of your day.

We agree to have a wordless love exchange once a day and to search for new wordless ways to say "I love you."

Signed _____ and _____

New silent ways to express love.

_____

_____

_____

_____

_____

_____

_____

As you discover new silent ways to express love to each other write them in the box above.

Enrichment Activity #2: Planting Seeds of Love®

Wordless love is fun, nevertheless it is important to learn to speak the language of the heart. Working together may make this easier. Try the following method to break the ice.

The goal is for you and your spouse to compose a joint love note. Begin by writing one word on the first line in the box on the next page. Then trade books with your spouse who will write a second word right next to the word you wrote. Repeat this sequence until the two of you have composed a statement or a profession of love in both books.

Tasteful humor is acceptable. Aim for 4-6 exchanges (8-12 words). Begin with simple easy goals. Don't expect to write the world's most romantic love note on your first try. It may happen but don't expect it!

Our First Joint Love Note

_____

_____

_____

_____

When you are finished, share your thoughts and feelings about the activity. Now you are ready to plant a *Seed of Love,® which* is simply a love note like the one you just created. You plant it by leaving it where your spouse will be sure to find it. Some examples include; in a purse or wallet, under a pillow, in the car or in a drawer.   It can be humorous, romantic, serious or tastefully teasing. You can keep replanting, adding one word each time as described above, or each spouse can write an entire note.

Seeds of Love® give your **Reservoir of Love** a triple infusion. It generates loving thoughts and feelings in you as you write it and again when your spouse finds it and expresses gratitude for your thoughtfulness. Your spouse will also get a healthy dose of loving thoughts and feelings of appreciation which will trigger the **Cycle of Love** along with the **Cycle of Appreciation**. Furthermore it delivers again each time either of you recalls the event. Love is so easy to generate, and always pays such tremendous dividends.

Now sign the pledge on the next page (in both books) that commits both of you to plant a *Seed of Love®* at least once a week. Once harvested be sure to store them in your **Midnight Harvest Treasure Chest.**

I promise to plant at least one *Seed of Love* ® **every week.**

Signed _____ and_____

Afterthought

 Over 27 years ago, Tricia and I began planting *Seeds of Love.*® This evolved into the loving dialogues that were published as a collection; **Midnight Harvest: Living in the Moment of Love.** The introductory verses of each session were adapted from this book. We discovered that the more we thought and wrote about love the more meaningful and love centered our relationship became.

We began choosing romantic places for the exchanges, and our relationship evolved into a series of romantic adventures around the globe. This simple practice started over a quarter of a century ago, continues to pay generous loving dividends to our marriage. We have never seen it fail to generate oodles of love and romance for anyone who has tried it. It will work for you too.

SESSION FOURTEEN (Litany of Appreciation)

For groups:

- For maximum effectiveness, please read through the entire session and review the general guidelines in the introduction prior to beginning the session.
- Select a volunteer couple to read the introductory poem. Let the couple decide who will read the opening verse and who will read the reply. After the reading, ask several volunteers to share their favorite lines, images, thoughts and feelings about the poem.
- Discuss the 5:1 ratio for a successful lifetime relationship and the importance of expressing appreciation toward one another as a way of preserving it.
- Ask volunteers to share some of the nice things that their spouses have done for them recently and then instruct couples to complete Part One of the **Litany of Appreciation** on their own.
- Remind couples that we rarely receive recognition for all the things we do and that it's important to ask for the recognition we want. Instruct them to continue with Part Two of the exercise.
- Lead a general discussion about what couples have discovered by doing this exercise, and then remind them they need to continue expressing appreciation and asking for recognition until it becomes a habit.
- Remind everyone of the importance of following the suggested maintenance schedule and encourage them to try a family appreciation session.

Evening Prayer

May we never yield to sleep
With unshared love in our hearts
Or an un-given kiss on our lips.

May our last thoughts be of one another
And the joys we shared.
In slumber's sweet embrace
May our hearts dance in love filled dreams.

Reply

With all my heart and soul
I join in your prayer
And if this be slumber's dream
May I never wake.

Detail of Painting by Toulouse Lautrec- Musee d'Orsay- Paris   **Photo by Frank Hajcak**

Reflection

Research consistently indicates that couples who stay together have more positive, loving thoughts about one another, and more supportive interactions and words with each other than couples who divorce. Some researchers report that a ratio of 5 positive for every negative thought, word, or interaction is necessary to sustain a healthy happy relationship. Think of this for a moment. Every negative, unpleasant, angry, or annoyed thought or word you have with or about your spouse should be counterbalanced with five pleasant, supportive and loving thoughts, words or interactions.

No relationship is perfect. Occasionally we all encounter cloudy weather. Just as a financially prudent person builds cash reserve for rainy days, a prudent loving couple builds a **Reservoir of Love** to preserve the 5:1 ratio through tough times. One of the best ways to insure that your 5:1 ratio will remain firm during unpleasant times is through appreciation.

Everybody loves to be appreciated, and it seems no one gets as much as they'd like. Lack of appreciation is the number one complaint of married couples, the number one reason people give for leaving their jobs, and the number one reason for separation and divorce. Thus, lack of appreciation is a block to the natural flow of love.

Appreciation lets your spouse know that you noticed, that you are pleased, that you care, and that you respect the efforts made to maintain the relationship. Showing appreciation is so effective because it creates a cycle of feelings similar to the **Cycle of Love** described on page 16. Studies show that when you express appreciation to others they feel pleased that their efforts were noticed. In turn they want to return the good feelings so they do more to please you.

Enrichment Exercise: Litany of Appreciation

In the space provided, list all the things that your spouse has done in the last few weeks that you noticed and appreciated. It's usually easier to start with recent events and work backwards. Be sure to remember the small things because they are the ones that seem to go unrecognized.

As you make your list, focus on the good feelings that thinking about these deeds generates in you. This list is called your **Gift List**. Give this list to your spouse. **But before you do**, complete the task in part two.

GIFT LIST

Part 2

In the space provided, list all the things you do for which you wish you would receive recognition and appreciation from your spouse. This is called your **Wish List**.

WISH LIST

Before you pass your Gift List and your Wish List to your spouse please note!

This is neither a contest for best spouse nor a time for criticism or resentment. If you receive a very short Gift List, it simply means that your spouse needs to acquire better observation skills. Thus, if you gave your spouse a short Gift List and your spouse gave you a long Wish List, it means **you** must work on your observation skills. **Thank** your spouse for helping you to realize this, then discuss ways you can increase your attentiveness. **Now make the exchange.**

Read and compare the two lists you just received. Were you surprised by how many or how few items were on either list? Discuss your reactions, what changes each of you would like to see and what actions need to be taken so that both of you will get the results you want. Remember this is a joint effort to generate more love and appreciation for one another. **Write your conclusions in the box below.**

```
┌─────────────────────────────────────────────────────────────┐
│  _____  │
│  _____  │
│  _____  │
│  _____  │
│  _____  │
│  _____  │
└─────────────────────────────────────────────────────────────┘
```

Appreciation needs to be given and received every day. It keeps you and your spouse tuned into what makes your relationship work. When both of you express appreciation you make one another feel good because both of you are getting and receiving recognition for the efforts that each of you make to keep the love flowing.

We used to advise a weekly ritual for exchanging gift lists. However, many couples reported this activity had a very positive effect on their relationship. We now strongly advise couples to make it a daily ritual. We like to call this daily ritual, the **Litany of Appreciation**.

Most couples find it works best to incorporate the **Litany of Appreciation** into their bedtime routine. Just before lights are turned off, one spouse begins naming things that were noticed and appreciated that the other spouse did. Begin each statement with, "I appreciate that you did _____." Try to think of everything your spouse did during the day that you thought was helpful and that you appreciated. The other spouse listens without interruption. Then switch roles.

The second spouse starts by saying; "I'm glad that you noticed so many things." Then begin the litany. End the ritual by both spouses confirming how good it feels to be appreciated.

 Please note: Sometimes the litany is short, sometimes it's long. If you did something for which you'd like appreciation and your spouse didn't mention it, simply say, "I'm very pleased you noticed and appreciated all those things. I also did _____." After which your spouse will reply, "I am glad you reminded me. I do appreciate that too."

THE NIGHTLY LITANY OF APPRECIATION IS THE BEST AND MOST EFFECTIVE SLEEPING AID IN THE WORLD. IT WILL SEND YOUR HEARTS OFF DANCING IN LOVE FILLED DREAMS.

If you're too tired at bedtime or have different schedules, another good time to share is at dinner. Many couples have turned **The Litany of Appreciation** into a family affair by allowing the kids to join in. Dinner time was turned into a **FAMILY FESTIVAL OF APPRECIATION** that everyone enjoyed. This is a great way for children to learn how to keep a loving relationship happy and healthy.

Afterthought

Considering that lack of appreciation is the number one cause of so much dissatisfaction, and realizing how easy it is to forget the little things during an entire week, we urge you to adopt a daily **Litany of Appreciation**. If you're serious about reaching soul mate status, sign the pledge below in both books!

We want to insure that we will reach soul mate status. Therefore we agree to have a daily Litany of Appreciation.

Signed_____ and _____

Hibiscus   **Watercolor by Julie Vollmer©2009**

Time Line for Love   **Photo** by **Frank Hajcak**
Taken through the clock in the cafeteria at the Musee d'Orsay in Paris.

SESSION FIFTEEN (Time Line for Love)

For groups:

- For maximum effectiveness, please read through the entire session and review the general guidelines in the Introduction prior to beginning the session.
- Select a volunteer couple to read the introductory poem. Let the couple decide who will read the opening verse and who will read the reply. After the reading, ask several volunteers to share their favorite lines, images, thoughts and feelings about the poem.
- Encourage a few couples to share with the group some of the unusual circumstances that brought the two of them together.
- Then instruct everyone to work independently on the time line for love, up to their marriage. From there finish it as a couple.
- When the activity is complete, ask couples to share some of their highlights with the group. Finish by reminding them that adding new events which highlight their love as well as reviewing the past events helps to keep their **Reservoir of Love** filled.
- Remind everyone of the importance of following the suggested maintenance schedule and to store additional events in their **Midnight Harvest Treasure Chest**.

Genesis

You came into my life
A miracle born of the breath of God
Gifted with love's vision.
Like a queen bestowing her blessing
My name rolled off your lips.
Like courting dolphins breeching the surface in slow motion
We break through time and enter the kingdom of love.

Reply

Gentle as the touch of a feather from an angel's wing
You came into my life – a flower born of starlight
Your fragrance filling me with unearthly joys
I could not fathom.
Your breath whispering visions of love
I could not imagine.
The paths of our pasts mingle like the threads of a tapestry
Woven by love flowing from the heart of heaven.

Reflection

There are no coincidences in life. Everything happens for a reason. Every event we experience connects and fits into the patterns of our life which in turn connects and fits into the patterns of the community, country, culture and world in which we live. Yet every one of us is unique and we all form our own special patterns that fit within the grand design.

The most important, special and unique patterns we create are those in our marital relationship. The types of interactions couples have with each other will influence their personality development and determine the course their relationship will follow. The patterns you develop from the activities in this program will keep you on course to the soul mate bond.

Unfortunately we tend to lose sight of the specialness and importance of our martial relationship as we become absorbed in ordinary daily routines. The first step for appreciating and preserving the specialness of our relationship is to understand how it fits into the overall grand design.

Enrichment Activity: Time Line for Love

Couples are to work independently of each other. Make a timeline of all the events that had to have occurred so that you and your spouse would meet and fall in love. Start with where you were when you met and work backwards. Be thorough and creative. Include small and big events. Be sure to include hobbies, interest, skills or talents that may have played a role in meeting or falling in love.

For example, say you met at a college basketball game. You both had to be in college and interested in basketball or social networking at that exact time. You both had to do well enough in high school to get into that college. What made the two of you choose the same college? You both had to obtain the financial resources to pursue your careers in this manner. Examine each detail to see how they connect to other events.

When you have exhausted all the possibilities, share your work with your spouse. Then together work forward from the time you met until your wedding. Again, be thorough and creative. Include as many events as either of you can remember. The more events you tie into your timeline, the easier it will be to see that:

"The paths of our pasts mingle like the threads of a tapestry
Woven by love, flowing from the heart of heaven."

Please note! Some couples think that because they lived next door to each other there are no unusual events that lead them to their soul mate. The fact that out of billions of people the two of them were born right next door to each other is one of the most incredible events that can happen on this planet! Furthermore how their lives slowly became intertwined undoubtedly involved several unusual events.

Events Leading to Our Wedding

We met

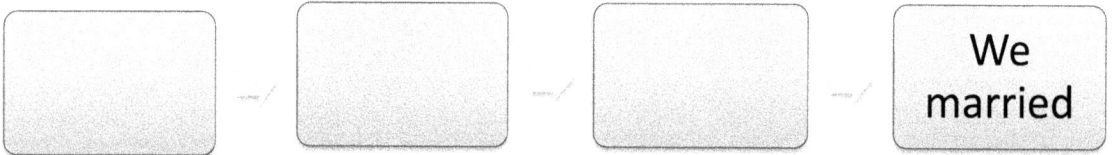

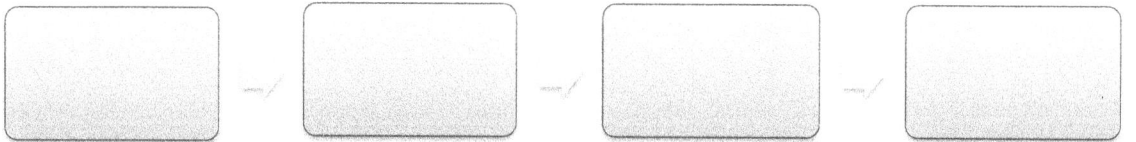

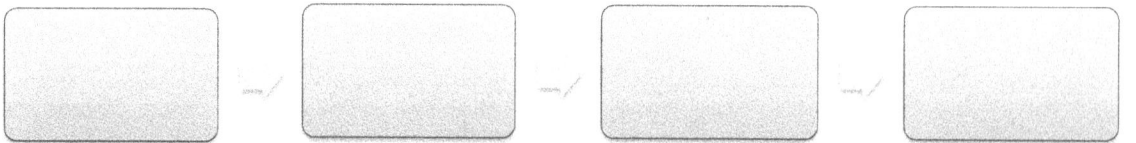

When you complete the timeline, share your feelings about how each event fits into and helps to shape the overall pattern, especially the ones that seem like a one in a million possibility. Summarize your reactions in the box below.

 Continue your timeline by adding special events that keep the fires of love burning bright. This will turn your timeline into a historical record of your journey to the soul mate bond. Read and sign the pledge below in both books.

> **We agree to record events that make our relationship special and brimming with love on 3x5 cards as they occur, store them in our Midnight Harvest Treasure Chest and have an annual review of *Our Time Line for Love*.**
>
> **Signed_____ and _____**

Afterthought

Many couples enjoy reading the timeline as part of their anniversary celebration every year which makes perfect sense. After all, you are celebrating the fact that you found each other and share something very special.

Entrance-St. Stephan's Church-Mainz, Germany   **Photo** by **Frank Hajcak**

SESSION SIXTEEN (Entering the Cathedral of Love)

For groups:

- For maximum effectiveness, please read through the entire session and review the general guidelines in the introduction prior to beginning the session.
- Select a volunteer couple to read the introductory poem. Let the couple decide who will read the opening verse and who will read the reply. After the reading, ask several volunteers to share their favorite lines, images, thoughts and feelings about the poem.
- Have a group discussion on which qualities, virtues, or personality traits focus on moral or spiritual development. (Honesty, Piety, Charity, etc.) Write them on an easel tablet for all to see. (Save this list for Session 20 on page 89.)
- Instruct couples to fill in the boxes and complete the enrichment activity.
- Instruct couples to sign the agreement to integrate spiritual beliefs into their emotional bond.
- Remind everyone of the importance of following the suggested maintenance schedule and to record any new material on 3x5 cards which should be stored in their **Midnight Harvest Treasure Chest**.

Soul Mate Kiss

Lost in enchantment between eyes and lips
Our hearts filled with the sweet wine
Of love that cannot be undone
Lays bare the empire of the soul.

Reply
Love guides the heart
To the empire of the soul
Your words are the pathway.

Reflection

Spiritualized, romantic, poetic imagery opens the door to new ways to see and to feel love. The spiritual dimension of romantic love is a vast new universe to explore. It offers hundreds of new ways to say "I love you." The deeper and stronger your spiritual beliefs are, the more ways you will discover for expressing love to each other and the stronger, more stable your relationship will become.

Spiritualizing romance with *Romancing the Soul along with the Heart®* creates the core of soul mate love and insulates your loving relationship from the stress of daily life. The previous session opened the door to spiritualizing romance by suggesting that more than the forces of emotional and physical attraction were involved in finding your soul mate. Now you can bring that force into your relationship.

Enrichment Activity: Entering the Spiritual Domain

Sit on the floor facing your spouse. In the box below list all of the personality traits of your spouse that go beyond physical characteristics and can be viewed as a pathway to the soul. For example, physical beauty and youthfulness fade with age but kindness, piety, and generosity tend to grow with age. (You can pick some from the suggestions generated by the group discussion but be sure to add you own ideas.)

```



_____


_____


_____


```

Next close your eyes and contemplate the goodness and vastness of these qualities. Consider how they transcend time and unite the heart to the soul. Think of these qualities as vast areas to explore and discover new ways to generate loving thoughts and feelings for each other.

When you open your eyes, without saying a word, gaze into each others' eyes. Think of the eyes as "the windows of the soul." Stare beyond the eyes and feel yourself being drawn into, surrounded and touched by feelings strong and deep. This is "the love that knows no Amen." As the feelings grow stronger, allow your heads to be drawn together until you are touching cheek to cheek. Whisper in each other's ear; "I love you, soul mate."

In the box below, independently describe your reactions, thoughts and feelings about the experience. When you are finished trade books and share them with your spouse.

Share any comments you wish and return the books. Now you are ready to make a commitment to take responsibility for courting the soul and the heart together, which simply means viewing your romantic thoughts and feelings about your spouse through a spiritual framework. The next few sessions will get you started.

Sign the pledge below, in both books, to affirm that both of you agree to make courting each other's soul and heart a theme in your relationship.

We agree to integrate our emotional love bond into our spiritual beliefs by courting the soul and the heart together once a month.
Signed_____**and**_____

Afterthought

The more often you look at your romantic loving experiences through your spiritual framework the more new ways you will discover to love each other and the stronger and faster your soul mate bond will grow. In addition, each time you do your **Reservoir of Love** receives an infusion of **emotional love and spiritual love**.

Rose Window-Notre Dame-Paris, France   *Photo by Frank Hajcak*

SESSION SEVENTEEN (Exploring the Cathedral of Love)

For groups:

- For maximum effectiveness, please read through the entire session and review the general guidelines in the introduction prior to beginning the session.
- Select a volunteer couple to read the introductory poem. Let the couple decide who will read the opening verse and who will read the reply. After the reading, ask several volunteers to share their favorite lines, images, thoughts and feelings about the poem.
- Review the concepts of spiritual love and how love for one another can lead to more spiritual love. Supplement with some of your favorite passages from Scripture or other spiritual writings.
- Start the activity by listing 4-6 primary spiritual beliefs of the group. Encourage couples to write them in their handbooks prioritized according to the personal value they feel toward each.
- Brainstorm together on how everyone can apply two or three of the spiritual beliefs to strengthen their love bond.
- Encourage couples to continue the work on their own.
- Remind everyone of the importance of following the suggested maintenance schedule and to record any new material on 3x5 cards and store these cards in their **Midnight Harvest Treasure Chest.**

Cathedral of Love

Love surrounds us like a cathedral
Blessing our pilgrimage
To the altar where love begets love
Shattering the boundaries between heaven and earth.

Reply

Through the vision of the soul
We are blessed with
New ways to see
New love to harvest
New paths to follow
Leading to heaven's door.

Reflection

It's time to tap into the power of your spiritual beliefs. The stronger your beliefs, the more they will enrich and strengthen the soul mate bond. It is the combined strength of **your and your spouse's** spiritual beliefs that determine the degree of enrichment and sense of permanence the relationship will acquire.

As with emotional love you can generate as much love in the spiritual realm as you wish. Simply connect one of your spiritual beliefs to one or several of your romantic thoughts or experiences. The more often you do this, the stronger you connect with your spouse, and the stronger a connection you form with the love that flows from the heart of heaven.

Enrichment Activity: Exploring the Spiritual Domain

In the box below, list two or three of your spiritual beliefs that are important and meaningful to you. For example, two basic Christian beliefs are the belief in God and the belief in an immortal soul. **(This activity is compatible with all faiths and spiritual beliefs. Your spiritual advisor will be glad to help you.)**

```
_____

_____

_____
```

Now brainstorm with your spouse and discuss how each belief can strengthen your marital bond. For example, the *Time Line of love* suggests that a higher power orchestrated your journey to find your soul mate. Thus completing the time line can help you feel more certain that your relationship was meant to be and that your love will last. Other examples of how the belief that possessing an immortal soul can enriche your relationship may include the following:

- Every interaction in your relationship affects your soul or spiritual welfare.

- Believing that you have an immortal soul can increase your motivation to be more loving and considerate to one another.
- Your belief that your soul is the foundation for building a love that will live beyond the physical world will motivate you to create and share more love.

In the box below, write a few notes that capture the highlights of your discussion on how your spiritual beliefs will strengthen your soul mate bond.

```
_____

_____

_____

_____

_____

_____
```

Now sign the pledge below in both books.

We agree to continue exploring, through monthly discussions, how our spiritual beliefs can enhance our relationship and increase our love for one another and record them on 3x5 cards to store in our Midnight Harvest Treasure Chest.

Signed _____ **and** _____

Afterthought

If you feel uncomfortable or unqualified to pursue this type of activity on your own we strongly suggest that you discuss your discomfort with your spiritual advisor.

SESSION EIGHTTEEN (Romancing the Soul and Spiritual Seeds of Love)

For groups:

- For maximum effectiveness, please read through the entire session and review the general guidelines in the introduction prior to beginning the session.
- Select a volunteer couple to read the introductory poem. Let the couple decide who will read the opening verse and who will read the reply. After the reading, ask several volunteers to share their favorite lines, images, thoughts and feelings about the poem.
- Explain that the activities in this session will intensify their connection between romantic love, emotional love and spiritual love.
- After they have finished the first activity, re-read the last line of the poem and challenge couples to think of ways to love one another more.
- Some couples may feel hesitant to try the *Spiritual Seeds of Love*® activity. It may be helpful to have the group do one or two first in order to build individual confidence and group enthusiasm. Then instruct couples to work on their own.
- When they have finished, ask a few volunteers to share one of their new creations.
- Emphasize how these activities add a powerful sense of permanence to their relationship.
- Close by reminding couples that they now need to look at one another every day as a special gift from their Creator and express their gratitude through loving interactions.
- Emphasize the importance of pursuing this activity as suggested in the Maintenance Schedule.

Corner of Creation

You stand so perfectly
In a special corner of creation
Ankle deep in stars
As if the Deity said
"Let there be grace and beauty and love."
What gift can I offer
In gratitude for you?

Reply

Like music from a star at the dawn of creation

Love reigns in heaven

And led me to your soul.

What thanks can we give but to love even more?

Reflection

Love is our direct connection to God. When couples integrate their spiritual beliefs into their relationship by courting the soul and the heart together, they strengthen their connection to God and to each other with every loving interaction they have. Through loving thoughts, words or interactions you express appreciation and gratitude to each other and to the Deity.

Our spiritual beliefs can also be used to intensify our romantic and emotional feelings and experiences. This next activity will demonstrate how this is done. We will use the belief that all humans have a soul and that life is a gift from the Creator.

From this perspective, your spouse is the creator's special gift to you who will help you achieve a level and intensity of love you could not reach on your own. The more this spiritual belief permeates your relationship the greater the degree of permanence your emotional love will attain. Take a few moments to appreciate this special gift.

Enrichment Activity: Courting the Soul

In the space provided, fill in the blanks with everything that you like about your spouse. You may copy from the list you composed on page 12 or 38. If you do, be sure to add any new ones that come to mind. This is your **Spiritual Gift List**. Some examples might include:

- Your eyes are God's special gifts to me.
- Your loving personality is God's special gift to me.
- Your smile is God's special gift to me.

Your _____ is/are God's special gift to me.	
Your _____ is/are God's special gift to me.	
Your _____ is/are God's special gift to me.	
Your _____ is/are God's special gift to me.	
Your _____ is/are God's special gift to me.	
Your _____ is/are God's special gift to me.	
Your _____ is/are God's special gift to me.	
Your _____ is/are God's special gift to me.	
Your _____ is/are God's special gift to me.	
Your _____ is/are God's special gift to me.	
Your _____ is/are God's special gift to me.	
Your _____ is/are God's special gift to me.	
Your _____ is/are God's special gift to me.	
Your _____ is/are God's special gift to me.	
Your _____ is/are God's special gift to me.	
Your _____ is/are God's special gift to me.	
Your _____ is/are God's special gift to me.	
Your _____ is/are God's special gift to me.	
Your _____ is/are God's special gift to me.	
Your _____ is/are God's special gift to me.	

When you are finished, trade workbooks and read what you have received from your spouse. Share your reactions by writing a brief note in the box below. Then return the books.

_____

_____

_____

_____

Discuss some ways you might show appreciation for your special gift. (**Hint:** reread the reply poem.) Be specific about how you will love more. For example, you might state, "I will read the Spiritual **Gift List** I just made, at least once a week." Make a note of any ideas the two of you produce and sign the pledge in both books to continue one of the ideas on a regular basis.

Ideas for generating more love as gifts of gratitude for each other.

_____

_____

_____

_____

We agree to use one of our ideas for generating more love as gifts of gratitude for each other on a _____basis. (Determine your own frequency.)

Signed_____ and _____

Enrichment Activity # 2: *Spiritual Seeds of Love®*

Couples report that the *Seeds of Love®* activity on page 54 is their favorite way of courting the heart. You can turn a seed of love into an instrument to court the soul and the heart together. Simply take a romantic, loving thought and add a spiritual framework based on your beliefs. Here's an example of how it can be done using the belief that God created the universe and endowed each of us with an immortal soul.

First, consider your beliefs about creation and the universe. You may envision billions of stars, the creation of your spouse, and all of creation as a work of love. Give thanks to the creator.

Next, combine these thoughts with an expression of love or admiration you feel toward your spouse in a way that also reflects and respects your spiritual beliefs. This combination creates the charm and loving nature of spiritualized romance. Some examples:

- He created billions of stars. One outshines the others – you!
- Since I met you, my prayers have changed … "Our Father, I am in Heaven. Thank You!"
- God said, "Let there be love," and you were born.
- Through our love for each other, we pay homage to God's love for us.

In the box below, write your own *Spiritual Seed of Love.®* As a last resort, you can borrow from the ones above, but you must add or change a few words to give it your personal touch.

```
┌─────────────────────────────────────────────────────────────────┐
│                                                                   │
│              My First Spiritual Seed of Love®                     │
│                 Date _____                             │
│                                                                   │
│   _____   │
│                                                                   │
│   _____   │
│                                                                   │
│   _____   │
│                                                                   │
└─────────────────────────────────────────────────────────────────┘
```

When you are finished, trade books and read what your spouse wrote. Share your reactions on the lines provided on the next page.

_____

_____   _____

The beauty of romancing the soul is that it opens the door to an infinite number of new ways to generate loving thoughts and feelings toward your spouse. *Spiritual Seeds* of *Love* ®are an ideal way to court the soul and the heart together. They are fun! Commit to having fun using them as you work to complete the soul mate bond. Sign the pledge below in both books.

We will alternate exchanging a *Spiritual Seed of Love* ® **one week and a** *Seed of Love*® **the next week.**

Signed _____ **and** _____

Afterthought

Completing these activities means that you acknowledge and accept your spouse as a special gift from the Creator. Seeing each other in this light adds a powerful, stabilizing force to your relationship and insulates it from petty daily stress. Now take the next step and ask yourself, "How should I treat this special gift?"

There should be but one answer which is, *"With love, respect and kindness."* Remind yourself to do so by printing the following sentence on a 3x5 card. Keep it on your desk or refrigerator where both of you will see it often.

"When I am kind and loving to my spouse, I am thanking my Creator
for this special gift to me!"

SESSION NINETEEN (Romantic Spiritual Imagery)

For groups:

- For maximum effectiveness, please read through the entire session and review the general guidelines in the introduction prior to beginning the session.
- Select a volunteer couple to read the introductory poem. Let the couple decide who will read the opening verse and who will read the reply. After the reading, ask several volunteers to share their favorite lines, images, thoughts and feelings about the poem.
- Ask if there are any problems viewing loving thoughts or feelings through a spiritual framework.
- Ask volunteers to tell how they are beginning to court the heart and the soul together.
- Explain that poetic imagery creates a comfort zone that stimulates the imagination and builds a bond between the heart and the soul.
- Ask couples to find four images from the poems in **Midnight Harvest: Living in the Moment of Love** which capture the spiritual and emotional nature of love and personalize them as in the examples given.
- Ask a few volunteers to share the original lines and the new lines they have created.
- Have couples sign their pledges to continue the search for images that court the heart and soul together.
- Remind everyone how important it is to follow the suggested maintenance schedule and to record any new material on 3x5 cards to store in their **Midnight Harvest Treasure Chest**.

Divine Love

Prophets spoke of love
Born of heaven's womb:
Stars fueled by love
Leaping through the night
Like twin constellations
Touched by the hand of God.
Personified in your soul
Heaven bless that I may deserve
The golden glow of starlight
Held in your heart.

Reply
We must follow our hearts
For heaven's hand shall
Guide us from star to star
Bathing our souls with love
That knows no Amen.

Reflection

Poetic imagery with a spiritual core is an ideal catalyst for bonding the heart and soul because it speaks to you on both an emotional and spiritual level. The spiritual aspect of the image courts the soul and lets you experience the depth and sense of permanence of the spiritual realm. The romantic aspect of the image courts the heart and lets you experience the personal intensity of the emotional realm. *Romancing the Soul along with the Heart®* lets you experience the power of both realms simultaneously. As the two realms become integrated, they influence one another.

The emotional realm acquires a stronger sense of stability and longevity from the spiritual realm. The spiritual realm acquires a more intense sense of immediacy and personal meaning from the emotional realm. Once integrated, they transform a simple emotional relationship into a profound soul mate bond.

In a few words, a poetic image with a spiritual core catapults you into the heart of soul mate love and lets you experience the unity of heart and soul with an intensity that would take pages, possibly books, of prose to accomplish. The power from this unity is harnessed every time you read spiritualized romantic poetry. This is why we recommend weekly or monthly readings from **Midnight Harvest: Living in the Moment of Love**. (The Psalms, Song of Solomon and other spiritualized works are also effective.)

Enrichment Activity: Romantic Spiritual Imagery

Working separately, go through the poems from **Midnight Harvest: Living in the Moment of Love** and find four phrases or images that you feel capture the spiritual and emotional aspects of love. Write them in the box on the next page.

Phrases or images that capture the spiritual and emotional nature of love

1._____

2._____

3._____

4._____

Next, trade books and share them with your spouse. Circle the number of the two from your spouse's list that you like the most. Then return books. Working as a couple, personalize the four images (two from each book) by adding words or phrases of your own that both of you feel puts your fingerprints on it. Some examples might be:

"We like to think of our souls as being cleansed by warm spring rains."
"We picture ourselves as courting dolphins swimming to the kingdom of love."
"We really like the thought of heaven's hand bathing our souls with the love that knows no amen."

Write your personalized responses in the box below.

Next, discuss and share any thoughts or feelings you experienced as you courted the soul along with the heart. Exchange ideas on how you can use romantic and spiritual images to enrich your relationship. Write a few highlights of your discussion and any conclusions you may have reached in the box below.

```
_____

_____

_____
```

Sign the pledge in both books, in the box below, to continue the search for images that connect emotional and spiritual love, once a month. (You can search together or independently of one another.) You may pick images or phrases from poems, love songs or romantic stories and add your own spiritual thoughts. Write them on a 3x5 card and plant it as a *Spiritual Seed of Love*®. Once harvested store it in your **Midnight Harvest Treasure Chest.**

> We pledge to search for and share romantic images that will connect our love to the spiritual world and plant it as a *Spiritual Seed of Love*® once a month.
>
> **Signed**_____ **and** _____

Afterthought

 The romantic and spiritual worlds connect in thousands of different ways. For example, a rose symbolizes love. It also reflects the beautiful intricacies of creation and can inspire spiritual as well as romantic thoughts, words or deeds. Use your imagination to create connections that are meaningful to you. Write them on a 3x5 card. Use them as *Spiritual Seeds of Love*® *as described above.*

Detail of Painting by Claude Monet - Musee d'Orsay, Paris   **Photo** by **Frank Hajcak**

Session Twenty (Setting the Course to Soulmate Love)

For groups:

- For maximum effectiveness, please read through the entire session and review the general guidelines in the introduction prior to beginning the session.
- Select a volunteer couple to read the introductory poem. Let the couple decide who will read the opening verse and who will read the reply. After the reading, ask several volunteers to share their favorite lines, images, thoughts and feelings about the poem.
- Before couples complete the first part of the activity, review the list of moral/spiritual virtues from session 16. Add new ones anyone wishes to contribute.
- Before couples map out their distance from the destinations, show them a sample on an easel pad or whiteboard.
- Have couples sign the pledge and set goals that will help them reach their destination.
- Emphasize how important it is to follow the suggested maintenance schedule and to record any new material on 3x5 cards to store in their **Midnight Harvest Treasure Chest**.

Heart to Heart

As if from the spell of love's dream
Angels whisper our names
And with golden thread
Bind us heart to heart
Soul to soul
Opening the door to soul mate love.

Reply
Breathing secrets of love you entered my soul
Each word a spark with the heat of the sun
Lighting the course to the kingdom of love.

Reflection

Think of your relationship as a ship on a journey to the soul mate bond. You and your spouse are the captains. You need a destination and a map. Otherwise you will have little chance of reaching your port (the soul mate bond). So let's get started.

Enrichment Activity: Setting the course

Working as a couple, list five qualities, traits or virtues that you think would facilitate achieving soul mate love. You can pick from the list produced by the group or name your own.

PRIORITY	TRAITS

Next, choose the three that both of you think are most important. Some examples might include: Piety, Hope, Charity, Kindness, Patience, Love etc. Write the three traits you both agreed upon inside the ovals below with the most important one in the top oval. These three ovals represent your destination or port of call.

You are here.   **Port of Call**

In order to plot your course, you need to know where your relationship is now. Let's find out. Using the above illustration, make three small ovals on the opposite side of the rectangle, under **You Are Here.** Write the same traits inside these small ovals in the same order as the larger ovals.

However, your placement must reflect your present relationship. The more of a trait you feel exists in your relationship, the closer to the port of call the oval should be placed. Connect the small ovals with their counterparts on the right as in the illustration below. Now your map is complete.

Later redraw it on a separate 8 ½ x11 sheet of paper. It will be easier to work with during your quarterly checkups. Some couples personalized it with small boats and little islands. Feel free to do so if you wish. Keep it in your **Midnight Harvest Treasure Chest**.

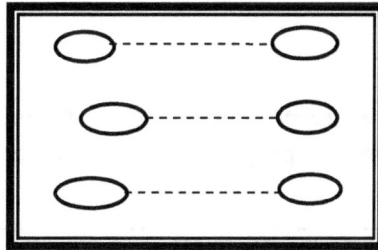

Please Note: This is a cooperative effort, not a contest for **Most Virtuous Spouse**. It does not matter who practices how much of a virtue. It is the combined effort that both of you put forth that matters. Simply make a subjective estimation of how much of the virtue you and your spouse already practice in relation to how much you both think is needed for a soul mate bond. The greater the gap, the further from the port of call your ship should be placed.

Discuss your feelings about your location on your map and things you can do that will get your relationship closer to your destination. Write two specific things in the box below.

Two things we will do to reach our destination:

1._____

2._____

Track your progress every three months. Place a small circle on each of the dotted lines at a distance that reflects the gain you made on each virtue. Write the month and day below these new circles.

Then share thoughts and feelings on how good it feels to see your progress. If no progress has been made, discuss specific ways to overcome any obstacles you may have encountered as well as ways to get back on track.

 Remember, no accusations or recriminations are permitted. This is a joint project. Cooperation and encouragement are the keys to success. The more time and effort you put into this activity, the more progress you will experience. This exercise is your map that will keep you on the path to the soul mate bond.

Sign the pledge below in both books to do this crucial quarterly maintenance activity.

We pledge to record our progress to soul mate love every three months.

Signed_____ and _____

Afterthought

Soul mate virtues are a joint project toward which both must work. Spouses should encourage one another and build on each other's strength. The goal is to live a love centered life. To guide your efforts adopt the attitude, from *Wisdom to Live By*:

"Walk softly and carry a big heart."

SESSION TWENTY-ONE (Legacy of Love)

For groups:

- For maximum effectiveness, please read through the entire session and review the general guidelines in the introduction prior to beginning the session.
- Select a volunteer couple to read the introductory poem. Let the couple decide who will read the opening verse and who will read the reply. After the reading, ask several volunteers to share their favorite lines, images, thoughts and feelings about the poem.
- Discuss the legacies that some ancestors of group members have left.
- Recount one or two of your favorite examples of legacies from scripture or church history.
- We generally think of legacies as something we leave to the world after we pass on, but in this activity you will **now** create the legacy you want to leave, so that you can live up to it **and** you will have served as an example for your children.
- Have couples complete the activity.
- Encourage open discussion about the legacies some couples have created and goals they have set to make sure they reach them.
- Emphasize how important it is to follow the suggested maintenance schedule for this activity.

Returning

Events cannot tarnish
Time cannot weaken
The love we create
Heart bound to heart
Soul to soul
Backed by the ancient pool of love
To which we all must return
Adding our offering
So our children may find their way
Through the darkness between the stars.

Reply
Our lives form a story of closeness and grace
Blessed beyond dreams
Flowing through galaxies
Carrying the ancient code of love
That began and ends at heaven's door.

Reflection

Eventually, everyone's time on earth will come to an end. Every moment you are alive, you are building your legacy. Your legacy determines how your family will remember you, what they will say about you, and what they will think about you after you are gone. Everyone leaves a legacy, yet so few give it serious thought. Fewer still, realize that everyone can leave the exact legacy they desire. However, keep in mind, the sooner you start planning it, the more likely you will achieve it.

Contemplating the brevity of life is a powerful motivation to begin building your legacy **now**. What better legacy is there than a life filled with millions of loving moments that you shared with those you love? As the poem states, the legacy that really counts is our:

> *"Offering to the pool of love to which we all must return*
> *So others (our children) may find their way*
> *Through the darkness between the stars."*

Through poetic eyes, we learn that loving interactions between parents are the role models children need most. This is the key to passing love from one generation to the next.

Enrichment Activity: Create Your Legacy

Working independently, create your own legacy. Begin with the question, "How do I want my family and spouse to remember me after I'm gone?" This is not a confession of short comings, so don't eliminate a quality because you think you fall short. For example, you may want to be remembered as a sensitive, romantic soul mate, but you can't remember the last time you gave your spouse an impromptu gift. Add it to your legacy anyway. Regardless of your track record, your legacy should characterize you as you want to be remembered not necessarily as you are now. The idea is to create a positive legacy, one you're willing to work toward fulfilling.

Now write your legacy in the box below.

```
┌─────────────────────────────────────────────────────────┐
│                        MY LEGACY                          │
│  _____      │
│  _____      │
│  _____      │
│  _____      │
│  _____      │
│  _____      │
│  _____      │
│  _____      │
│  _____      │
└─────────────────────────────────────────────────────────┘
```

Share your legacy with your spouse. **Please Note: No accusations, judgments or criticisms allowed!** Only encouragement is permitted. Read what your spouse wrote. Then write your encouraging comments on the lines provided below.

_____

_____

_____

Now return books and brainstorm together how you can help each other live up to the written legacy. Be specific. Start by one spouse asking the other, "What can I do to ensure that you will remember me this way." Ask the same question for each characteristic you want your spouse to remember about you.

In the box below, write the steps and resolutions you have made to ensure that you will live up to your legacy.

Path to My Legacy

_____

_____

_____

_____

_____

_____

_____

_____

_____

In both books, on the next page, sign the pledge to have a joint quarterly check-up on your progress toward reaching your goals. Set a date for the first check-up. Keep in mind that even though you each created your own legacy, fulfilling it is a joint project. You must work together by recognizing and appreciating each other's efforts and by brainstorming together about how to overcome any obstacles either of you may encounter.

> **We agree to check our progress and help each other to fulfill our legacy goals every three months.**
>
> **Signed** _____ **and** _____

Now set the date for your first check-up on this line. _____

Afterthought

Hint: The most effective way to help people become the kind of person they want to be is to treat them as if they already were that person.

Say your spouse wants to be remembered as a considerate person. Whenever your spouse does something that was motivated by consideration for another person's feelings or needs, pile on the praise and appreciation. Be sure to make a connection between what your spouse did and how your spouse feels as a result of the action.

For example, say one of the kids is frustrated putting a model air plane together and your spouse helps solve the problem. Try saying, "You handled that situation very nicely. You must feel good that you were considerate and helpful." Do this consistently and it will become a self fulfilling prophesy.

You may even drop hints to get the ball rolling. For example, "Gee Hon, Chris is having a tough time adjusting the bicycle seat. If you offered to help, I'll bet (s)he would be grateful and think you were a very kind and considerate person.

SESSION TWENTY-TWO (Ode to Love)

For groups:

- For maximum effectiveness, please read through the entire session and review the general guidelines in the introduction prior to beginning the session.
- Select a volunteer couple to read the introductory poem. Let the couple decide who will read the opening verse and who will read the reply. After the reading, ask several volunteers to share their favorite lines, images, thoughts and feelings about the poem.
- Discuss the importance and challenge of living a love centered life every day.
- Explain **Ode to Love** journaling and its importance in facilitating the love centered life. Encourage couples to keep the journal and sign the pledge in both books.
- After everyone completes the exercise, have an open discussion for couples to share which activities they liked and found most helpful.
- Emphasize how important it is to follow the suggested maintenance schedule for this activity.

So This is Love

So this is love
The kind that's beyond dreams and fantasy
That makes you dance and sing like Cinderella
So this is love
The kind you're afraid to wish for more
Because you might implode into tiny bits of star dust
And end up in another galaxy
Where the only thing you know
Is the voice inside your head
Singing of love that sends seismic shivers
Through your soul
Casting spells that make stars collide
Creating black hole gravity
From which there is no desire to escape
So this is love,
The kind you brought into my life.

Reply

Yes this is love
The kind that makes you feel like you're standing
On the edge of the universe
Drinking in the light of a trillion suns
Savoring the moment love was born,
Living that moment – every moment
Sharing it with soul deep understanding
Sheltered by Heaven's door.
Yes this is love,
The kind you brought into my life.

Reflection

The strength of every soul mate bond is determined by the combined power of a couple's emotional love **and** their spiritual beliefs. The spiritual aspect insulates, protects and preserves the emotional bond which in turn personalizes and intensifies the spiritual bond. Thus they form the core of the soul mate bond that allows you to:

> **"Live in the moment of love- every moment-**
> **Sharing it with soul deep understanding-**
> **Sheltered by Heaven's door."**

You enter the moment of love by taking ownership of your relationship and performing the maintenance responsibilities that will integrate your loving experiences with your spiritual beliefs. When you do this, love becomes the driving force in your life, and it has but one purpose; **to create more love**. The more love you create, the more stable your life becomes because love will permeate every aspect of your relationship.

Enrichment Activity: Ode to Love

The key to entering the moment of love lies in ***Ode to Love*** which is a journal of all the loving events, interactions and experiences you had during the day. This will keep you focused on love and all the loving experiences you share with your spouse and family.

Keeping a journal of Love is a very rewarding experience. It's a daily reminder of how wonderfully enriching love feels and how peaceful and unifying love is. It will generate many loving thoughts and feelings as you write in your journal. It will also keep love flowing through all your interactions and into your reservoir. The more experiences you record the more stability your relationship will acquire.

Furthermore, journaling about love strengthens your relationship because each entry activates the **Cycle of Love.** Thus, it not only adds more love to your reservoir but also preserves your 5:1 success ratio for lifelong love. It's like doubling the effectiveness of your investment of time and energy. Therefore, the more effort you put forth, the sooner you will achieve a love centered life.

 Likewise, the more spiritualized romantic events you record the more the emotional and the spiritual realms will integrate. It is these two realms working together that create the drive to love more which is the force that lies at the core of the soul mate bond.

Keeping Your Journal

At the end of the day, find a quiet place to work for about 10 minutes. Take a mental walk backwards through the day and record every loving thought, word, and deed you can recall. Be sure to include the goodbye and welcome home hug or kiss, any loving thoughts of appreciation, the love note you may have written, and anything else that made your life more love oriented. Once a week share your journal with your spouse. This will reignite the love cycle and generate more love for your reservoir.

Some couples reported they:
- Carry a notepad and record loving thoughts and events as they occur.
- Include these events in the Litany of Appreciation.
- Include the kids in a daily or weekly family session so they can share their experiences of love.
- Several couples have reported that their kids were inspired and motivated to start their own journals. **This is an ideal way to teach children about love and how it makes life more pleasant.**

Usually within six months, focusing on love becomes a habit and you will automatically seek out loving interactions. **Love begets love**. Eventually it will permeate all aspects of your relationship and become the stabilizing force in your life. **Ode to Love** only takes about ten minutes a day. Are you willing to commit to this task? **Write your answer here.**_____

If you wrote "yes," begin right now. In the boxes provided below, list three activities from these sessions that helped you think about love in a new or different way and two that helped you to see your spouse in a more loving light.

1._____

2._____

3._____

1._____

2._____

Trade workbooks with your spouse. Share any thoughts or ideas you have on what each of you read or wrote. Then, write the essence of what you discussed and shared in the box below.

_____

_____

_____

_____

_____

Next, read and sign the commitment in the box below, in both books.

We agree to spend _____minutes a day keeping our *Ode to Love* journals which we will share once a week.

Signed _____ and _____

Now set a date by which both of you will have purchased a journal for keeping your Ode to Love. Record it on this line._____/_____/_____

Afterthought

The **Litany of Appreciation** keeps you focused on what is working and having a positive effect on your relationship. **Ode to Love** keeps you focused on creating, expanding and sharing love. Working together they are an unending source of fuel for lifelong love. Many couples have developed a weekly **Family Celebration of Love** where everyone shares and expresses appreciation along with their loving thoughts and feelings.

Print the quote below, from *Wisdom to Live By*, in large bold letters on a 3x5 card and use it as a book mark for your **Ode to Love** journal.

"The amount of love you create and share throughout life becomes your solace in your twilight years."

SESSION TWENTY THREE (Living a Love Centered Life)

Note to session leader:

- The final session is a wrap-up, and you should read the scenarios below prior to the session.
- Begin this last session by reading **So This is Love,** from the previous session. Then read the reflection to the group. Next, have a 5-6 minute silent reading session during which the group members read and compare the two scenarios. (If you prefer volunteers can take turns reading a paragraph or two to the group.)
- Then discuss the following points:
    1. The difference between the love centered and the typical life is determined by the attitude a couple has as they follow the Maintenance Schedule.
    2. Simple things like *Seeds of Love®*, **Litany of Appreciation** and **Ode to Love** will keep couples focused on love and what makes their relationship work. Once they become habits, love automatically becomes the center of their life.
    3. This will have a positive impact on their family life and will be an excellent template for their children to follow.
- Next, read **The Decision** to the group.
- Instruct couples to sign the pledge to follow the maintenance schedule on page xiii.
- Hold the closing ceremony during which the group forms a circle and you read the poem, ***How Do I Love Thee?,*** to the group.
- Have a closing blessing.
- We highly recommend that you schedule a follow up session within 4-5 weeks where couples bring in their journals and share their favorite practices and activities.
- Be sure to close with a reminder of the connection between accepting responsibility and gaining power. We like to close with: **Congratulations! You have all accepted the responsibility for your relationship and have gained the power to control it and create all the love you need to form a soul mate bond. Now go and exercise the power you have acquired.**

Reflection: The Love Centered Life

You are now equipped to create all the love you need to form a soul mate bond and live a love centered life. The poem, ***So This Is Love,*** captures the romantic intensity of what this is like. The best way to understand in practical terms what it is, how it works and how it changes your life is by comparing the following two scenarios.

THE ROAD MOST TRAVELED: A Typical Event

Relieved the day is over; you wrap things up at the office. You begin to feel tense as you walk to your car, anticipating rush hour traffic. As you get in the car, you're blinded by the sun low on the horizon. Annoyed, you slap down the visor. As you drive, the stress of the sun and traffic combines with the leftover anger from the disagreement you had with your spouse this morning. You start ruminating and thinking, "How could some who loves you say something like that? My spouse doesn't care about my needs and doesn't realize how hard I work!"

You are cruising on the highway at 55. Suddenly, without signaling, a slow moving car pulls out in front of you. You slam on the brakes and stop inches from the car. Now all the negative feelings gush out of control. "That idiot could have killed me! … didn't even signal… must be crazy!" You work yourself into a rage for the next 10 minutes.

You arrive home upset. Your children's bicycles and skateboards are blocking the garage entrance. Your negative rumination continues. "I told them a million times never to leave their toys there. Just like Chris, they never listen." You jump out of the car and yell, "That's it! You're all grounded!"

You start to really feel sorry for yourself as you think, "I was almost killed, and this is the welcome I get. I could die, and they probably wouldn't even notice." You half snarl a hello to your spouse who snaps back at you. "Why are you yelling at the kids? You just got home. They couldn't possibly have done anything to deserve that." You snap back. "You always take their side. You don't care about me." And this morning's argument starts all over again.

THE ROAD LESS TRAVELED: The Love Centered Life
Here's how the same scenario unfolds when you apply the activities you learned in this manual.

You wrap things up at the office relieved that the day is over so you can go home to your haven from the business world. You recall that you had an unpleasant interaction with your spouse this morning and feel a little distressed. You start ruminating about the argument, so you take the **Admiration List** out of your wallet and follow the procedure. You conclude with, "My spouse is such a wonderful gift to me." You feel confident the issue will be resolved, regain your positive orientation and proceed to your car.

The sun blinds you as you sit in your car. You flip the visor down. A little blue card falls from behind it and lands on your lap. You recognize it as a ***Seed of Love***® your spouse planted a few weeks ago. You smile as you read it to yourself, "Somebody loves you." It's your favorite, signed by the whole family. You keep it there as a reminder of their love. As you drive and think about the closeness of your family, you feel very blessed and lucky.

The same near accident unfolds on the highway. You stop inches from the car's bumper. Similar angry thoughts pop into your mind. "That idiot could have caused a serious accident." But your pool of positivity generated by the **Admiration List** and the ***Seed of Love***®, keeps you focused on the bright side of things as you think, "Lucky I have been blessed with such fast reflexes. Someone up there must be watching out for me. I can't wait to get home to my family where I feel safe and loved."

Although a little tense, you arrive home in an upbeat mood and find the garage blocked with toys and the kids engrossed in play. Your positive orientation continues as you comment to yourself, "Looks like they're having so much fun that they forgot about the rules." You get out of the car, run to the children, give them a hug and say, "Glad you're having fun, but where do these toys belong?" You smile as they put their things away and feel that your family is gifted with love.

You enter the house and greet your spouse pleasantly. You share an embrace as you look out the window admiring the children. Both of you are confident they will inherit the **Legacy of Love** you are planning to leave them. You relate the close call you had on the way home as you both prepare the dinner. Tonight, the **Litany of Appreciation** will have a few deep moments of closeness and your entrants into **Ode to Love** will express gratitude for all of the blessings and love received this day. This week end's **Family Celebration of Love** promises to be the best ever.

The Decision: Choose Your Life Style

Which life would you prefer? Choose **The Road Less Traveled** and love will become the dominant, stabilizing force in your life. The more love you create using the activities in this manual, the faster your **Cycle of Love** will automatically stop negative ruminations, distractions and other obstacles to love. There will be less room for negativity, anger, hate and divisiveness in your life. Your family will function as a loving unit and your children will acquire loving habits they will pass on to their children.

When you live a love centered life you start changing the world one family at a time. Others will notice your example, and follow. Most important, your children will see how wonderful and unifying love is and follow in your footsteps. As we say in *Wisdom to Live By*:

"Get children hooked on where you want them to go and they will find a way to get there."

The products from these activities that you have stored in your **Midnight Harvest Treasure Chest** will be their map. Your **Ode to Love** journal will be their guide.

Now you have to make the most important decision of your life. You stand at the intersection of the road that leads to a love centered life and the road that leads to trusting in luck and hoping for the best. Which road will you take? The choice is yours.

Decide NOW! Sign the pledge to follow your hearts and live in the moment of love that remains untarnished by events and undiminished by time, sheltered by heaven's door.

Date_____

We will follow our hearts and lead a love-centered life by following the Maintenance Schedule in the front of the book on page xiii.

Signed _____ and _____

Closing Ceremony

Groups: Instruct couples to form a circle and hold hands. Have a minute or two of silence while couples meditate on the power gained by taking responsibility for their relationship **and** the power generated by integrating the emotional and spiritual aspect of love **and** their ability to create all the love they want. Instruct them to allow these thoughts and feelings to fill their mind, body, heart and soul. After the pause the group leader reads: **HOW DO I LOVE THEE?** (From: *Midnight Harvest: Living in the Moment of Love.***)**

Individual Couples: Spend a minute or two contemplating the power gained by taking responsibility for your relationship **and** the power generated by integrating the emotional and the spiritual aspect of love **and** your ability to create all the love you want. Allow these thoughts and feelings to fill your mind, body, heart and soul. Then read the poem to one another as if you are blessing each other with love that flows through your heart from the heart of heaven.

How Do I Love Thee?

How do I love thee?
Let me count the ways.
As eagerly as the honeybee enters the first flower of spring
And the morning glory greets the dawn,
As gently as the sun kisses away the morning dew
And the moon reflects the sun,
As completely as the sky enfolds the earth
And night surrounds the stars,
As passionately as the virgin's first love
With a depth and breadth expanding each moment beyond measure.
Thus shall I love thee
'Til the breath of life no longer flows.
Then joined by choirs of angels
I shall love thee even more.

Reply

My heart, quivering with love can find no words
To greet thy pledge.
I shall bask in the joy of a love so gentle
Eager, passionate and complete
'Til my soul is overfilled
and repay thee each day a-hundred fold,
'Til life no longer flows.
Then joined by myriads of angels
We shall love forevermore.

Closing Blessing

AFTERTHOUGHTS

The key to a successful, enrichment encounter is follow up. One encounter by itself will get you off to a good start. To keep the momentum going, couples need to have follow-up contact. We recommend:

1. Right now schedule a follow up session in 4-5 weeks for couples to bring in their journals and share their favorite practices and activities.

2. Get volunteers to set up a web site or blog where couples can exchange ideas, share results and encourage each other to keep on the path to soul mate love.

3. A large scale annual retreat for all participants from this and former groups is a very effective follow-up and can also serve as a support group.

Every church should have a spiritual advisor or counselor that can be a valuable resource for the spiritual integration process.

Parting Thought

You have accepted the responsibility for your relationship and have gained the power to control it and the power to create all the love you want to form a soul mate lifelong bond. Now go and exercise the power you have gained.

Give Your Friends the Gift of Lifelong Love

Midnight Harvest: Living in the Moment of Love

The complete collection of loving dialogues, enhanced by 33 illustrations, celebrates 30 years of romancing the soul along with the heart. Vivid verbal and visual imagery captures experiences couples will encounter as they journey to the soul mate bond and live in the moment of love untarnished by events and undiminished by time.

Romancing the Soul along with the Heart®
The Secret of Lifelong Love

Thirty heartwarming and soul-bonding activities for couples to generate spiritualized romance, acquire the power to change their relationship and form a lifelong soul mate bond. A convenient maintenance schedule validates the lifetime warranty for living in the moment of love.

Both available at Amazon.com and other retailers.

Future Works

Seeds of Love and Spiritual Seeds of Love: Hundreds of love notes (Seeds of Love® & Spiritual Seeds of Love®) for *Romancing the Soul along with the Heart.® Includes instructions* for personalizing them or using them to jump start your imagination to create your own. Plus dozens of Meditations to enlighten and guide the heart on the path to the soul mate bond.

Wisdom to Live By: Manual for using over 100 original insights for Romancing the Soul along with the Heart,® and keeping you focused on designing the life you were meant to live.

Soon to be available at Amazon.com and other retailers.

Visit their website- **FrankHajcak.com**

About the Authors

Frank Hajcak, Ph.D. and **Tricia Garwood**, MS maintained a joint private practice and consulting firm specializing in self-empowerment and relationship enrichment in the Philadelphia area for over 25 years. Their first book, on sustaining long-term relationships, was the main selection of the **Psychology Today**, the **Psychiatric and Social Science** and the **Behavioral Science** book clubs and has been translated into French, Polish, and Estonian and featured in *Glamour* magazine.

Frank and Tricia have co-authored six books and dozens of magazine and journal articles. They have lectured and given workshops throughout North America. Both are also noted for their work and publications in art and photography. They reside in Florida where they offer workshops and classes in creativity, photography and relationship enrichment.

For more information visit their website- FrankHajcak.com

Special thanks to Joy for her insightful suggestions, enthusiastic support and encouragement.

Joy Shelton, B.A. is the founder-director of **Sprinkles of Joy** Ministries, and a member of **CLASS (Christian Leaders, Authors, Speaking Services)**. For the past 35 years, she and her husband **Rev. Marvin Shelton** have served many churches in Louisiana, Kentucky, Indiana, Pennsylvania and Florida. Joy has also served as a **Family Ministry Consultant** for the **Louisiana Baptist Convention.**

Organizations and institutions that provide relationship enrichment services receive special discounted prices on bulk orders.

Contact: HumanPotentialPress@yahoo.com

*Notes:*_____
_____
_____
_____
_____
_____
_____
_____
_____
_____
_____
_____
_____
_____
_____
_____
_____
_____
_____
_____
_____

*Notes:*_____

_____

_____

_____

_____

_____

_____

_____

_____

_____

_____

_____

_____

_____

_____

_____

_____

_____

_____

_____

_____

_____

_____

*Notes:*_____

*Notes:*_____

_____

_____

_____

_____

_____

_____

_____

_____

_____

_____

_____

_____

_____

_____

_____

_____

_____

_____

_____

_____

_____

_____

Notes:_____

_____

_____

_____

_____

_____

_____

_____

_____

_____

_____

_____

_____

_____

_____

_____

_____

_____

_____

_____

_____

_____

*Notes:*_____

_____

_____

_____

_____

_____

_____

_____

_____

_____

_____

_____

_____

_____

_____

_____

_____

_____

_____

_____

_____

*Notes:*_____

_____

_____

_____

_____

_____

_____

_____

_____

_____

_____

_____

_____

_____

_____

_____

_____

_____

_____

_____

Notes:_____

_____

_____

_____

_____

_____

_____

_____

_____

_____

_____

_____

_____

_____

_____

_____

_____

_____

_____

_____

*Notes:*_____

_____

_____

_____

_____

_____

_____

_____

_____

_____

_____

_____

_____

_____

_____

_____

_____

_____

_____

_____

*Notes:*_____

_____

_____

_____

_____

_____

_____

_____

_____

_____

_____

_____

_____

_____

_____

_____

_____

_____

_____

*Notes:*_____

_____

_____

_____

_____

_____

_____

_____

_____

_____

_____

_____

_____

_____

_____

_____

_____

_____

_____

_____

Notes:_____

_____

_____

_____

_____

_____

_____

_____

_____

_____

_____

_____

_____

_____

_____

_____

_____

_____

_____

_____

*Notes:*_____

*Notes:*_____

_____

_____

_____

_____

_____

_____

_____

_____

_____

_____

_____

_____

_____

_____

_____

_____

_____

_____

_____

_____

*Notes:*_____

_____

_____

_____

_____

_____

_____

_____

_____

_____

_____

_____

_____

_____

_____

_____

_____

_____

_____

_____

_____

*Notes:*_____

_____

_____

_____

_____

_____

_____

_____

_____

_____

_____

_____

_____

_____

_____

_____

_____

_____

_____

_____

_____

www.ingramcontent.com/pod-product-compliance
Lightning Source LLC
Chambersburg PA
CBHW050353100426

42739CB00015BB/3387